Our Lives Matter

Our Lives Matter

A Womanist Queer Theology

Pamela R. Lightsey

PICKWICK *Publications* · Eugene, Oregon

OUR LIVES MATTER
A Womanist Queer Theology

Copyright © 2015 Pamela R. Lightsey. All rights reserved. Except for brief quotations in critical publications or reviews, no part of this book may be reproduced in any manner without prior written permission from the publisher. Write: Permissions, Wipf and Stock Publishers, 199 W. 8th Ave., Suite 3, Eugene, OR 97401.

Pickwick Publications
An Imprint of Wipf and Stock Publishers
199 W. 8th Ave., Suite 3
Eugene, OR 97401

www.wipfandstock.com

ISBN 13: 978-1-4982-0664-8

Cataloguing-in-Publication Data

Lightsey, Pamela R.

Our lives matter : a womanist queer theology / Pamela R. Lightsey

xxiv + 104 p. ; 23 cm. Includes bibliographical references.

ISBN 13: 978-1-4982-0664-8

1. Black theology. 2. Sex—Religious aspects. 3. Queer theory. I. Title.

BT304.912 .L54 2015

Manufactured in the U.S.A.   10/26/2015

To Those Who've Gone Before: Lillie Mae Holmes Lightsey, Eddie Lee Lightsey, Darrell Darnell Lightsey, Sheila Lightsey and Torry K Lightsey Ross.

Every keystroke was made possible by your imperfect but unconditional love.

Contents

Preface

I AM A BLACK queer lesbian womanist scholar and Christian minister. To say that I am queer is not only my self-identity; it is also my active engagement against heteronormativity.[1] Indeed, queer ideology supports my long-held suspicion that sexual identity may not be as fixed as my generation was taught by society and the Church.

I want to be clear: I am not a disinterested observer writing for the sake of supporting some lesbian, gay, bi-sexual, transgendered, or queer (LGBTQ) friend, nor is this project motivated in light of the HIV/AIDS pandemic or any desire on my part to argue against the continued stereotypes that it is a "gay disease." Though both are worthy points of entrance, they are not the focus of my writing. Rather, this project is fueled by my personal passion for a subject with which I have an intimate connection: the plight of persons whose sexual orientation or whose behavior and appearance do not conform to traditional gender norms. In light of their plight, my plight, I have no right to give a passive, disinterested, voiceless treatise.

This is gut-wrenching, scandalous, debatable, yet also academic and practical work. Many who are familiar with my work will now likely question the very adjectives they once used to describe my work: *anointed* preacher, *brilliant* scholar, *effective* pastor, *Christian* disciple, *compassionate* counselor, *fruitful* evangelist. They will likely not easily grasp the possibility that God has been present and working through the life of a queer woman. Many will likely disavow every good work I have done, unable to reconcile my life and this writing with that of a "real" Christian believer.

---

1. Michael Warner coined this term in *Introduction: Fear of a Queer Planet*. He uses the term to describe and critique the cultural, institutional, and political governing that privileges heterosexuality as the essential, normative, and natural sexual identity for all humanity.

Some might say this book is a courageous undertaking. I do not. In fact, my earlier years of silence had been nothing less than cowardly. No matter how strongly I advocated—as pastor and as scholar—against homophobia and discrimination of the LGBTQ community, as a person I chose to remain distant. I rationalized my silence: *now is not the right time; you're a single mother who needs to feed her babies; don't shame your family, your friends, your church. . .*and on and on and on. I often told my LGBTQ peers, "The historic Church can be an evil place. Be careful." And I was careful. So very careful. Careful and miserable.

When I came out, I did so with both fear and a righteous passion for the liberation of others. As one who is not far removed from the conservative evangelical tradition, I know from first-hand experience what it is like to be ostracized because you disagree with denominational polity and how it feels to be labeled as the "the Other."

During my twenties, I was "silenced" by my pastor because I asked too many questions about the church's laws including those against women wearing pants and jewelry. This line of questioning was determined to be my stubborn resistance to the rules of our Pentecostal church and highly disrespectful to our female pastor. Being silenced meant I could not sing in the choir, teach, comment or ask questions during Sunday School, and I was denied the opportunity to stand and give my testimony during the highly regarded element of worship called "testimony service." What I had to say did not matter during the days of my punishment. I had said enough just by asking questions.

My pastor thought she was teaching me to be an obedient member. What I actually learned was a lesson that has helped make me the scholar I am today: A question can be both powerful and dreadful. It is not the answer but the act of asking simple questions that has helped shape me into on of the leading African American queer lesbian voices of social justice activism in the United Methodist Church. My relentless questioning has also led me to womanist theology.

In defining itself through the lenses of Alice Walker's *womanist* definition,[2] womanist theology has provided historically marginalized

2. Alice Walker, *In Search of Our Mothers' Gardens*, xi. Walker defines "womanist" in four ways, each with extensive differentiations, to include: "1) A black feminist or feminist of color 2) A woman who loves other women, sexually and/or nonsexually . . . sometimes loves individual men, sexually and/or nonsexually 3) Loves music . . . dance . . . the moon . . . the Spirit. . .love and food and roundness . . . loves struggle . . . the Folk . . . loves herself. Regardless and 4) Womanist is to feminist as purple to lavender."

Black women a platform from which to speak of both God and the Church in ways that set the "church captive" free. womanist theology gives Black women the theological resources to see themselves and the world in ways that do not privilege whiteness or patriarchy. Precisely because Alice Walker describes a womanist as "committed to survival and wholeness of entire people," and because womanist theologians have taken this element of the definition very seriously in their writings, I was attracted to womanist theology and have found its methodology most helpful for my theological research based on queer theory.

Walker's womanist framework allowed me to redefine my perspective of theology and sexuality with an attention to the wholeness and interconnectedness of all people. It was her definition of a womanist as "a woman who loves other women, sexually and/or nonsexually. . .sometimes loves individual men sexually and/or nonsexually" and its bold acceptance by some not all Black female religious scholars, that simply blew me away! I was stunned that Black religious scholars would use this definition given what I saw as the Black community's propensity to be extremely homophobic. Walker's definition is not merely about sexuality but also about love of the entire community, love of "the folk," and it was from that point that I began to focus on sexuality not merely within the realm of sex but from a much broader perspective of sexuality and the wholeness of the person as they are connected to all of God's creation.

Fortunately for me, I was able to study with three of the academy and Church's finest theologians while a student at the Interdenominational Theological Center (ITC) in Atlanta: Dr. Jacquelyn Grant one of womanist theology's premier scholars, Dr. Randall Bailey, a Hebrew Bible scholar whose work challenges not only the racism of Western theology but the homophobia of the Church, and Dr. Riggins Earl, Jr., an ethicist whose work argues against normative suppositions of race and class, which are so often and easily presumed valid. Their lectures challenged me to think within as well as outside the box. I learned to think within the box to understand provincial old-school churchy arguments. I was challenged to think outside the box designed by Western theology that depicts itself as "orthodox" and therefore the only "true" way of understanding God. I was inspired to study hard, well, and long so that I might intelligently identify both the strengths and the weaknesses of Western theology and therefore competently present an argument that does not deny the sacredness of persons who do not see themselves within the constructs of heteronormativity.

While I reveled in Womanist theology, at the end of the day I found it lacking. At the time too few womanist theologians had offered writings from other than heteronormative perspectives. With rare exceptions, LGBTQ womanist scholars have yet to offer critical scholarship at a time when our youth and young adults are keenly aware of minimal Black female theological scholarship on gender expression and sexual identity. They yearn to hear and read more from self-avowed Black LGBTQ theologians. They see and have been victims of the Church's oppressive teachings against LGBTQ persons and they yearn for the voices of more out Black LGBTQ scholars.

When I speak to young Black LGBTQ persons I remind them that just as coming out is not always safe in the greater society there has been a consistent pragmatic reality that coming out can be dangerous and can ruin a budding career within the academy. "We struggle against oppression all the time. Why give anyone ammunition to destroy a career you have worked years to build? What motivation has Black LGBTQ theologians who are often very connected to their churches (many quite theologically conservative) that would inspire them to risk their livelihood?"

I am thankful to see some changes and the presence of more out Black LGBTQ scholars in the academy. But it has been a painful season of progress. Having kept quiet, I have watched Blacks be far too slow to stand in solidarity addressing issues related to the lives of LGBTQ people. In the mid to late twentieth century, our white LGBTQ community and allies increasingly became more open and progressive on the matter, establishing healthy domestic relationships and advancing the political agenda of the movement. When I came out, I joined the ranks of a handful of out Black scholars but it was not because a handful was all that existed. We handful took the power of the question and placed our scholarship to the task of addressing homophobia within our Black churches and communities.

During the early part of this twenty-first century, as we began to see slow change within the academy we also found ourselves writing essays and resolutions to address same-sex-loving[3] relationships because of the political campaign that was launched to make same-sex marriage a major issue during George W. Bush's 2004 run for reelection against John Kerry. Democrats lost that election but by the time of the 2008 election the party was prepared to succeed against the divisive "wedge issue" strategy of the GOP. On a national level I began to see more and more Black leadership

3. Though the term same-gender-loving has been commonly used, I prefer to use the term same-sex-loving.

within the church and the academy showed their advocacy for same-sex marriage and human rights for LGBTQ persons. Black LGBTQ voices within the academy began to ask powerful questions concerned that our silence gives the appearance that we are not as concerned about social justice as we purport in our writings, lecturing and teaching. The powerful voices of self-identified Black queers and Black allies showed the Black LGBTQ community our desire to be authentically engaged against injustice and for some scholars it meant being open about their personal relationships in order to model healthy and loving relationship with loving partners.

As we celebrated the election of President Barack Obama, I turned my attention to the liberatory perspectives of womanist theology believing that it contained nuggets that might help me as an emerging queer activist. Now is the time for Lesbian, Queer, Intersexed, and Transgendered womanists to stand in solidarity on the values already set in place within womanist theology. Not the least of those values is *loving themselves and the folk*—the responsibility of being in right relationship with one another. To do so, we must be unashamed of our difference and willing to put our scholarship not so much "where our mouth is" but rather, *where our love is*. Womanist theology has been helpful in offering a foundation for womanist queer scholarship. My entry into queer theory and theology research has been inspired by womanist dialogue from which I continue to grow as a scholar and minister.

I have been in ministry for over 35 years. The last decade has been a lonely season—culturally speaking—because I am the only out African American ordained queer lesbian elder in the United Methodist Church. There are other out LGBTQ African American clergy, but none are self-identified lesbians, bisexual, transgender or queer who carry the credentials "ordained elder in full connection." Wish it were so, but not as of August 2015. We have any number of "semi-out" Black LGBTQ ordained clergy. They are out in small enclaves of the church and academy where it is safe to be out but are not out on a sustained national level. I don't write this to be received as a critique of them but rather a critique of an environment where people feel compelled to pick and choose spaces where they can be their authentic selves.

I chose to come out, fully, because I was spiritually suffocating in the closet. I was writing and speaking as an ally which always felt like I needed to limit what I said and that I could not use the full methodological resources and arguments consistent with being a womanist scholar. I spoke as a witness, an ally, a person who knew oppression because I was Black and female. I was ashamed and fearful of speaking from my true context: Black, female and queer lesbian.[4]

Most important, I have also come to this place for the sake of my daughter LaGeisha, son Dweylon, grandson Kedar, and goddaughter Treva. Children I raised to appreciate diversity and who have shown such courage in combating homophobia that I have been put to shame. They have little fear debating the subject of sexual identity in their college classes and communities in South Georgia, an extremely conservative area. Though their advocacy is no doubt in part because they are aware of their mother's queer nature, their commitment to pursuing difficult subjects through intensive research, intellectual rigor and critical reflection has been refreshing and gives me hope in the capacity of their generation to help usher in equal rights for LGBTQ persons much like their involvement in helping to elect the first Black president of the United States of America.

4. Later in this book I say more about my "queer lesbian" self-identity.

Acknowledgments

My CHILDREN AND FAMILY have supported my work and this manuscript. They and friends within the LGBTQ community have eagerly awaited its publication. I am thankful to them and to those who have helped me complete this short work that took many years of self-assessment, critical reflection and scholarly research. Phillis Sheppard, Renee Harrison, Thelma Haynes and Pansy Hammock have lifted me in prayer and encouragement when I thought I had no words for the despair I felt while writing about *bhomophobia* and the task of writing in general.[1] They have patiently read early iterations of this work and other similar essays. I am also thankful for my friends Da Vita McCallister, Andrea Fleming Whitehurst and my Lightsey-Leeks-Holmes family.

Monica Roberts provided essential advice as I wrote the chapter about trailblazing Black transwomen. Ulrike Guthrie has provided exceptional editing and displayed remarkable patience as I slowly authored this first manuscript. Many thanks also to colleagues and students at Reconciling Ministries Network, Garrett-Evangelical Theological Seminary, Boston University School of Theology, Union United Methodist Church and Broadway United Methodist Church. These places have helped me live with the questions so that I had the courage to do research and activism inspired by the questions.

Finally I thank the ancestors who comprise that great cloud of witnesses. I have felt their presence and have prayed for their assistance. For them and for the God of all Creation, I am much obliged.

---

1. A term I use to describe homophobia in Black churches and communities.

Abbreviations

LGBTQ   lesbian, gay, bisexual, transgender, queer

RMN   Reconciling Ministries Network

UMC   United Methodist Church

Introduction

As an African American queer lesbian womanist scholar, I am interested both in how post-structuralists have adopted the term *queer* and spun from it a field of study known as *queer theory* and in whether this subversive academic discourse might have some usefulness for my own womanist scholarship. Included in the womanist's several layers of meaning are womanist ways of loving "the folk" and one who is "committed to survival and wholeness of entire people."[1] This being so, one can make the case that womanist methodology that allows for the examination of categories such as race, gender, sexuality, and class is an excellent platform for doing queer theology. Particularly as these are womanist methodology's primary points of departure from Western theology, which is critiqued for being too often the perspectives of living and dead white men[2], the strength of this book is its utilization of womanist methodology to contextualize this work as useful for a broad range of persons.

On the other hand, just as I seek to offer this research to a large audience (because of the expansiveness of the LGBTQ community), I am aware that it has its own limitations because of my context as an ordained clergyperson in The United Methodist Church. Though readers from other faith traditions can learn about queer Christian theology using this text, as a Christian this book characteristically engages the central problems of the LGBTQ community using doctrines and dogma oriented not only

---

1. Walker, *In Search of Our Mothers' Gardens*, xi.

2. Here I am using a now familiar criticism of Western Theology. This is not to suggest that this project will not utilize relevant theological arguments ideas from any number of scholars. As a womanist I privilege the scholarship of womanist scholars but not to the irrational exclusion of helpful perspectives from other disciplines and systematic theologians. Some will no doubt see this as a type of intellectual fornication and yet it is consistent with the womanist way of declaring authority for ourselves.

by Christian theology and moral reasoning but especially by Wesleyan thought. Notwithstanding such doctrines as free will, the sacraments, and reconciliation, as a United Methodist clergyperson I'm especially influenced by this statement of an unknown source often erroneously attributed to John Wesley regarding the variety of opinions held by Christians: "In essentials, unity; in nonessentials, liberty; and in all things, charity." As a womanist scholar, I am ever seeking to display an attitude of charity with the hope of creating opportunities for dialogue that helps people survive and be made whole.

The methodology of this work draws upon three research foci: the collecting of narratives to develop empirical knowledge; intersectional analysis; and cross-disciplinary study. The empirical and contextual work of this project rests largely on collecting narratives and histories of Black women, as privileging the experiences of Black women is an important tenet of womanist methodology. This work does that in a way not heretofore accentuated in that it addresses most specifically Black lesbian, bisexual, transgender, and queer women. As an intellectual model, the methodology of this queer womanist work is concerned with producing knowledge for a broad audience and ensuring its epistemological validity. As a resource for social discourse, I believe the work of bringing to the fore the theological perspectives of Black LBTQ women is fertile ground for investigation. It is their voice that has largely been rendered silent or investigated inconsiderably through the lenses of heterosexual scholars (allies and opponents).

Not unique to womanist scholarship is this work's intersectional analysis that explores the impact of race, gender, class, gender identity, and sexual orientation on the theological understandings of LBTQ Black women. These points of departure from what some call "orthodox" Western theology remain critical to the work of womanist scholars because these subjects are significant to the peace and reconciliation of the peoples of this global world. The analysis is predicated upon an intersectional approach simply because it makes good scholarly sense. The disenfranchisement of women intersects with the disenfranchisement of Black men, of poor people, etc.; the disenfranchisement of Black lesbian women intersects with the disenfranchisement of transgender women, and so on.

This book will also be of concern to those who are neither Black nor Black women. Rather than reflect solely on the impact of oppression to Black queer women, this work will demonstrate, through experiential narratives and theological resource how the oppression of Black queer women harms the larger society. It does this by addressing both the intersections of minority oppression and also such oppression's nefarious impact on humanity.

Likewise, it is my delight to write in a manner that draws upon several disciplines. Interdisciplinary studies in areas such as sociology, philosophy, theology, and ethics have helped make sense of my own existential situation: that of being an African American female scholar, clergy, "former" heterosexual now self-identified lesbian–a queer living in America.

Several questions have come to my mind, which I will discuss in this book: 1) How does the experience of being a member of a distinctly oppressed group impact one's theological perceptions? And are those perceptions truly distinct? To do so, I will investigate the narratives of Black queer women holding them under a theological analytic lens that draws from resources such as reason and scripture. The goal is not to provide empirical data but resources for continued reflection and deliberation. 2) How may it be possible to live in harmony in the midst of distinctions among humanity?

I admit these are fairly rhetorical questions to which there are myriad possible responses. Nonetheless, they are not off limits from critical reflection. Now more than ever I am convinced they matter a great deal and to a great number of people, not simply to those of us whose vocation it is to "ask the deep questions."

I am also interested in the more nettlesome questions that serve as interesting challenges against using the term *queer*: 1) Does the definition and use of the term so radicalize its advocates that they end up segregating themselves from the rest of society? 2) Does the stance against heteronormativity equate to the rejection of the very systems/institutions to which advocates of queerness seek inclusion and/or civil rights?

The ongoing response to these questions has been to say that what makes "queer" (or queerness) so different is not only its adherents' use of the term to declare their unwillingness to be placed in stagnant sexual categories but also the term's *ambiguity* of definition. Is this ambiguity an intentional subtlety—perhaps since most of the ways we speak about sex/sexuality are ambiguous? What do we really know about sex and sexuality? Queer denotes ambiguity amidst sexual ambiguity. It is not an unwillingness to fully explicate or to rigorously declare a sort of epistemic privileging of defining queer identity. (Queer need not become an epistemic community.) Instead, like all humanity, we live as sexual beings that know little about the sex we enjoy. This is why I find queer theology so fascinating.

It allows for possibilities beyond my present understanding. It dispels the notion of expertise we often feel obliged to bear.

And yet there are some ways of identifying that as a writer I need for this project. For instance, for the sake of clarity in this work, my use of the term *same-sex loving* is not synonymous with *same-gender loving*. The former is characterized as an attraction to persons based on physical traits such as sexual organs, specifically breasts, penis, and vagina, while the latter is an attraction to persons who exhibit identifiable same-gender traits and performances culturally ascribed as either masculine or feminine and who may or may not have the same biological sexual markers. In short, a biological female might be attracted to a biological male only because that male's gender performance is feminine. The attraction this biological female has for this biological male thus falls under the same-gender-loving construct. Queer, eh?

As easily as I have made these distinctions, the use of the term *queer* does not always afford distinctions that are so simplistic. Queer is ambiguous not simply because it is being reclaimed in new ways but because it proposes that while sexuality is real, it should not be construed as necessarily taking one permanent form. To identify as queer is to assert a type of fluidity in life, particularly sexually. In fact, the fluidity of sexuality is the freedom of possibility, the possibility to be sexually attracted in multifarious ways. To wit, within the queer community there is a faction of persons who are unwilling to be restricted to one fixed gender identity or category of sexual behavior. They argue that such ambiguity is an essential trait of queer folk. Male or female, heterosexual or homosexual, act of birth or act of choice are all elements of the study of sexuality that has entered a new paradigm.

In this paradigm, sex is not synonymous with gender. That is to say that the presumed biological sex offers no material absolute conclusion for gender. Boys need not be masculine and girls need not be feminine in the sense of Western traditional expectation of heterosexual practice governed by gender categories. As the expectations of gender norms have been shattered by an ever-increasing presence of exceptions to the rules associated with biological sex, medical experts have had the questions put to them: *What is boy? What is girl?*

The questions have uncovered a simple truth: Sex cannot be assumed or prescribed merely by the presence of *external* sexual organs nor gender by biological traits. This simple truth has led to complex discussions regarding both sex and gender. During this era, queer persons argue that gender is the consideration of both sexual and cultural constructs that more often than not dictate normative behavior for the individual. Thus, we have come to see how powerful are the cultural norms that demand we live our lives with a binary presupposition of either man *or* woman and moving our bodies in acceptable masculine/feminine ways.

CHAPTER 1

Black Women's Experience
and Queer Black Women's Lives

WOMANISTS HAVE ALWAYS MAINTAINED the right to make claims about their experience and ways of knowing. As womanist anthropologist Linda Thomas put it: "the tasks of womanist theology are to claim history, to declare authority for ourselves, our men, and our children, to learn from the experience of our forebears, to admit shortcomings and errors, and to improve our quality of life."[1]

Womanist theology draws upon several sources including Black literature, personal narratives, and historical texts. According to womanist ethicist Katie Cannon, Black women's literary tradition has been the primary source for doing womanist theology: "the Black woman's literary tradition is the best available literary repository for understanding the ethical values Black women have created and cultivated in their ongoing participation in this society."[2] If this is the case, and I believe it is, the concern of queer womanists is why womanist scholars have given such sparse attention to the lives of LBTQ Black women. The answer is simple: Queer womanists must do the work.

Though womanist scholars have been exploring human sexuality for some time, they have not yet produced a full queer theology manuscript totally committed to the lives of Black lesbian, bisexual, transgender, and queer women. Black authors of fictional novels and queer theory have long

1. Thomas, "Womanist Theology, Epistemology, and a New Anthropological Paradigm," 38.

2. Cannon, *Black Womanist Ethics*, 7.

surpassed us in their critical analysis of the lives of Black LBTQ women. Of the academic articles and chapters published, only a small percentage are written by self-identified and publicly out LBTQ womanist scholars.

While this may or may not impact the overall validity of the work, I believe there is something noteworthy about a reader being able to pick up a book knowing it has been written by someone who has experienced and may therefore understand their situation. For instance, Jacqueline Grant's work, *White Women's Christ and Black Women's Jesus* (from which this chapter's title is adapted) resonated so strongly with me as a Black Christian woman because on the basis of her experience as a Black Christian woman she was able to tap into a way of knowing and understanding Jesus Christ that our white feminist colleagues could not. We are at a point at which there is clear interest in the subject of human sexuality and at which persons are looking for such writings by Black LGBTQ scholars.

Some might take this to suggest a kind of essentialism, that is not my intent. My insistence that we have more manuscripts by LBTQ womanists is precisely because I realize no one person can be that privileged voice for any group of people/culture. Every class of people is made up of diverse ways of being (i.e. Black lesbians in North America differ from Black lesbians in Africa). What I am suggesting is that the absence of Black lesbian, bisexual, transgender, and queer voices representing their unique perspective is not good for the academy or our churches, especially Black churches. I do not want silence to be interpreted by anyone as meaning Black LGBTQs do not exist, do not care, or have no impact in these contexts.

In this chapter, I will survey the work of several womanist scholars related to sexuality. In that they address general themes such as Black sexuality and the nature of Black homophobia, the writings of these avant-garde scholars are resources for the growing discussion about Black LGBTQ persons. Unfortunately most of these discussions talk about us and not with us. They rarely address the theological conception of Black LBTQ women in particular and our lives in our Black communities and churches. This means that even with the best intentions womanist scholarship has rarely put its finger on the pulse of what it means to be a Black lesbian, gay, bisexual, or transgender woman living in America.

Exploring the lives of any culture is good and necessary work. We need to learn from the experience of lesbian, bisexual, transgender, and queer Black women how the church has been helpful and harmful. We also need to discover how we as scholars can help train a new generation of clergy and faculty to affirm LGBTQ persons as people whom God loves as they live out their lives as same gender loving persons. To meet this task, Black LBTQ women must play a more immediate role in liberation theology by writing what it means to be queer bodies shaped in the image of God, by writing of our conceptions of God, and by writing against the oppression we face daily. Otherwise we run the risk of the history and theology of our people being shaped primarily from the perspective of our allies.

I am concerned not only with supplying our womanist colleagues, the academy, and the world sufficient literary and ethnographic repositories for their studies but that what comes from those studies is not a conflation of our experiences into *blackness* at the expense of our *queerness*. This of course is the well-documented critique Audre Lorde had of white feminist works, their "refusal to recognize those differences, and to examine the distortions which result from our misnaming them and their effects upon human behavior and expectation."[3]

With that in mind, what follows is an analysis of the few widely accepted full monographs written by womanists dealing in whole or part with the subject of LGBTQ sexuality or Black women's bodies: Kelly Brown Douglas' *Sexuality and the Black Church* and M. Shawn Copeland's *Enfleshing Freedom: Body, Race and Being*. Other monographs worth mentioning but not written by womanist scholars include: Horace Griffin's *Their Own Receive Them Not*, Roger A. Sneed's *Representations of Homosexuality: Black Liberation Theology and Cultural Criticism*, E. L. Kornegay's *A Queering of Black Theology: James Baldwin's Blues Project and Gospel Prose*, and Patrick Cheng's *Rainbow Theology: Bridging Race, Sexuality and Spirit.*

Kelly Brown Douglas' Sexuality and the Black Church

I remember the excitement at the Interdenominational Theological Center bookstore about Kelly Brown Douglas' work, *Sexuality in the Black Church*. It was a groundbreaking publication by a Black scholar on the subject of what we seminarians understood as sex. We passed the book around squealing with excitement, "Hey doc, you need to check this out!" Students stood in an increasingly long checkout line to purchase what was to us theological porn. A salacious book written about the Black Church! Many of us thought Douglas had written a tell-all about something we all knew existed—promiscuous and adulterous preachers. We couldn't wait to

---

3. Lorde, *Sister Outsider*, 114.

get the book home, set aside our dull readings written by dead white men, and read about Black preachers having sex. I was closeted at the time and wanted to read more about what she had to say about homosexuality. I hoped her work would help me to reconcile my relationship with the Protestant Church, but more importantly I needed to read from the pen of a Black theologian that I was not a sinner, an abomination in the eyes of God.

We'd be disappointed on the first count. Douglas had not written an exposé on the sexual exploits of Black clergy but a sustained investigation into Black sexuality. Her book is an exquisite survey of the history of oppression against Black bodies from slavery to its legacy of internalized oppression in contemporary America. Douglas' diagnosis of the impact of slavery and its continued consequences on black bodies is rich. Her work is especially helpful for Black women who have borne the brunt of racist attacks against their bodies.

On the second count, what Douglas had to say about homosexuality was trailblazing. Standing there browsing through the book, I almost cried knowing some Black theologian had actually put forth the effort to challenge homophobia within our Black communities. Douglas was one of few Black theologians who stood in solidarity with LGBT persons in the late '90s. Most Black academicians were either silent or anti-gay, and certainly this was true in womanist circles. In the introduction, Douglas notes the influence of lesbian scholar Renee Hill who, in her article, "Who Are We for Each Other? Sexism, Sexuality, and Womanist Theology," critiqued Christian womanists for avoiding "the issue of sexuality and sexual orientation by being selective in appropriating parts of [Alice] Walker's definition of womanism."[4] Not only Hill but also Black lesbian activist Rev. Irene Monroe had aptly critiqued this void in womanist writings at the time of Douglas' publication. *Sexuality in the Black Church* was a tiny step in the right direction but was not written to be a panacea for discrimination endured by Black LGBTQ people. Instead, what Douglas does beautifully, and what accounts for the continued worth of the book, is her treatment of Black sexuality, Black self-love of our bodies, and the nature of Black homophobia.

Though Douglas argues against a hyperhomophobic Black community,[5] the nature of Black homophobia is nonetheless patriarchal, Platonic, and hegemonic. Black church leaders, largely male, have so appro-

---

4. Douglas, *Sexuality and the Black Church*, 1.

5. Ibid., 89.

priated these traits that it is laughable to hear Black evangelicals take issue with the idea that homophobia in the Black community has been fueled by conservative white evangelicals. It is a bit of a stretch to suggest, as does Douglas, that Black Americans were not at all influenced by White biblical interpretation.

> Finally, the existence of the oral/aural tradition signifies that the Black community gives virtually no credence to White interpretations of the Bible, and for good reason. The way in which the enslavers used the Bible and the history of White biblical scholarship have caused many Black people to be suspicious of most biblical scholarship, of "book religion."[6]

It is true that early African Americans viewed White biblical interpretation with suspicion and even disregarded those passages of scripture that had to do with slavery and that were used as tools to justify their enslavement. Nonetheless, the doctrine of the inerrancy of scriptures dates back to the creeds of the early Roman Catholic Church, is carried forth in several confessions during the Reformation, and continues through Protestant denominations such as the Southern Baptists. Fiery revival preachers during the period known as the Great Awakening espoused the doctrine of the inerrancy of scripture, and we still find it articulated in some Black Protestant mainline and nondenominational church teaching. For example, at the time of Douglas' writing, the phrase, "God said it, I believe it, that settles it," a popular motto used by Billy Graham, could be seen hanging from banners in Black churches across the nation.

While Black Christians may be suspicious of white Biblical interpretation, they have not divested themselves of the influence of white Biblical scholarship, white evangelical perspectives, and the white prosperity gospel. Many Black preachers are theologically conservative thanks to the influence of white evangelicals such as Oral Roberts and Billy Graham. At the time of Douglas' publication, LGBT persons were hard pressed to agree that the "mistrust of White people's handling of the Bible runs . . . deep for Black people, who, as a result, find it hard to accept White renderings of biblical texts on any matter, including sexuality."[7] Black people then and now sat under the teaching of white pastors such as Ted Haggard, Jimmy Swaggart, John Hagee, Earl Paulk, were among the many who gathered to hear the preaching of evangelist Billy Graham and, need I recall, among

6. Ibid., 95.
7. Ibid.

those Blacks who followed Jim Jones to their deaths? Black homophobia is part of white sexual exploitation fueled by an uncritical acceptance not only of black but also of white preachers' biblical interpretation.

Reading *Sexuality and the Black Church* was therefore both a gift and a problem. Douglas' work emphasized that "human sexuality must be viewed as a gift from God."[8] Her work is one of few projects that said categorically that homosexuality is not sinful. She calls out the Black church and community for espousing a "sexual rhetoric that castigates gay and lesbian sexuality and/or admonishes gay and lesbian persons for experiencing the fullness of their sexuality."[9] Not only did she speak about sexuality, Douglas spoke about a major health issue of our time, HIV/AIDS. I was struck by Douglas' devotion to those living with HIV/AIDS. In fact, the pandemic of HIV/AIDS is her point of entrance into the theological treatment of sexuality. Unlike other apologists of the time, Douglas sought to disconnect the conversation about sexuality of LGBTQ persons from a medical crisis that many assumed was caused solely by homosexuality. She acknowledged, "The inappropriate association between HIV/AIDS and homosexuality has been perhaps the critical factor in causing Black passivity in regard to the AIDS crisis."[10] The problem was that Douglas did not say enough about this faulty association.

Sexuality and the Black Church was published at a time when gay men would have welcomed a more thorough critique of AIDS-related stigma. This prejudice directed against same-gender loving persons was detrimental to HIV education, prevention, and care. With HIV/AIDS known at the time as "the gay disease," the Church became a purveyor of gay bashing, with many notable clergy ranting about HIV/AIDS being a curse from God against "the abomination of homosexuality." The stigma made Black men painfully vulnerable, subjects of "you think he's got IT?" gossip, and seen as untouchable members within a culture where touching and hugging is commonplace and a demonstration of loving fellowship. Notwithstanding the unfortunately brief attention it gave to AIDS-related stigma, *Sexuality and the Black Church* was incredibly helpful as a theological resource within the Black community, especially for pastors in ministry with gay Black men who both feared contracting the disease and being branded as modern day lepers.

8. Ibid., 121.

9. Ibid., 127.

10. Ibid., 3.

Yet the book was so broad in its analysis of sexuality that it left many Black LGBTQ persons still yearning for a full discussion on the sexuality of Black LGBTQ persons. I am not suggesting the need to write a theology of Black LGBTQ sexuality that is little more than a pornographic treatise, but that something could have been said candidly and unabashedly about the gift of LGBTQ sexual *expression.*

M. Shawn Copeland's *Enfleshing Freedom: Body, Race, and Being*

The primary thesis and motive of M. Shawn Copeland's book, *Enfleshing Freedom: Body, Race, and Being,* was not to describe human sexuality. However, it is often used in Queer Theology courses because Copeland's theological anthropology of suffering Black women's bodies is done in such a way as to allow, nay demand, we hear its message for all bodies. It has been received among my Black LGBTQ friends as a breath of fresh air. We opened it with great expectancy and on completing it universally acknowledged what an excellent discourse on the body, specifically black women's bodies, she had framed. Copeland suggests that human bodies are, "the medium through which the person as essential freedom achieves and realizes selfhood through communion with other embodied selves."[11]

To date, Copeland's work is the only womanist manuscript that seriously addresses the sexual expression–sex acts–of LGBTQ persons. By asking two very poignant questions, Copeland helps the reader understand the dilemma LGBTQ persons have with Church teaching:

> This teaching admonishes gays and lesbians to repress or sacrifice their sexual orientation, to relinquish genital expression, to deny their bodies and their selves. But, if the body is a sacrament, if it is the concrete medium through which persons realize themselves interdependently in the world and in freedom in Christ, and if in Catholic sacramental economy "to express is to effect," then, on Catholic teaching, in and through (genital) bodily expression, gays and lesbians are compelled to render themselves disordered. For on Catholic teaching, the condition of homosexuality constitutes a transgression that approximates ontological status. Can

11. Copeland, *Enfleshing Freedom,* 24.

the (artificial) distinction between orientation and act (really) be upheld? What are gays and lesbians to do with their bodies, their selves?[12]

Copeland reflects rigorously and critically on human sexuality. She presents a sound Christology related to the body and helps LGBTQ persons anchor their place as members of the body of Christ. Yet, prior to the exceptional reflection noted above, Copeland is critical of defining sexuality only as genital sexual acts. She begins her critique by being mindful of the need for a healthy use of our sexual energies and drives and their integration within our spirituality. "A healthy appropriation of sexuality is crucial to generous, generative, and full living. A full embodied [sic] spirituality calls for the integration of sexual energies and drives, rather than repression or even sublimation."[13]

Copeland's beautiful embrace of bodily expression sampled in the passages above are preceded with an extensive section that lifts up Raymond Lawrence's critique of how we have "poisoned" eros. Copeland walks the reader through Audre Lorde's work to explore this point. I think it is important to take a look at Copeland's reading of Lorde and then at what Lorde actually wrote, not only for clarification but also as a helpful way of seeing how the implications of what Lorde wrote may be used in our work today:

> Copeland: We have poisoned eros, Raymond Lawrence contends. First, *we have substituted sex for eros,*[emphasis mine] then appropriated "a vision of sex as a fearsome and destructive force in human life." Audre Lorde echoes his assessment. In "Uses of the Erotic as Power," she maintains that we have confused eros with "plasticized sensation or with its opposite, the pornographic." Lorde seeks to release eros from the confines of the bedroom and to reconnect it with "lifeforce" and "creative energy." Eros, she proposes, is "the first and most powerful guiding light toward any understanding . . . the nurturer or nursemaid of all our deepest knowledge.

> Lorde: The erotic is a resource within each of us that lies in a deeply female and spiritual plane, firmly rooted in the power of our unexpressed or unrecognized feeling . . . The erotic has often been misnamed by men and used against women. It has been made into

12. Ibid., 75.
13. Ibid., 64.

> the confused, the trivial, the psychotic, and plasticized sensation. For this reason, we have turned away from the exploration and consideration of the erotic as a source of power and information, confusing it with the pornographic.[14]

Lorde counters the male illusion of power and instead situates eros as a *kind of power* within female grasp, for it lies within this "deeply female and spiritual plane."[15] Black LBTQ women especially need to understand their own internal sources of power and not allow them to be corrupted by anyone or any lover! Lorde clearly counters a misuse and misnaming of the erotic. However, I do not think that we should read Lorde to suggest she wants to remove eros from the bedroom but rather, as Copeland states, from the "confines" of the bedroom. That is, eros is not limited to the bedroom. As *the sensual*,[16] it may be expressed in any number of places, including the bedroom.

This may seem like a subtle point but it is very important for LGBTQ Christians. The majority of homophobic attacks against LGBTQ persons from the Christian Church are concerned with what we do with our genitals in the privacy of our bedrooms with our partners. That is, the Church is concerned with our sex, which it misnames as an "erotic deviant nature." Copeland's attention to eros helps us embrace again the powerful argument Lorde makes about our fear of the erotic–the sensual—because it connects the spiritual and the political. As pornography emphasizes sensation *without feeling*, so too we try to suppress our internal power, eros, and we fear our ability to "feel deeply all the aspects of our lives."

> The dichotomy between the spiritual and the political is also false, resulting from an incomplete attention to our erotic knowledge. For the bridge which connects them is formed by the erotic—the sensual—those physical, emotional, and psychic expressions of what is deepest and strongest and richest within each of us, being shared: the passions of love, in its deepest meanings . . .[17]

> This is one reason why the erotic is so feared, and so often relegated to the bedroom alone, when it is recognized at all. For once we begin to feel deeply all the aspects of our lives, we begin to

14. Ibid., 53–54.
15. Lorde, *Sister Outsider*, 53.
16. Ibid., 56.
17. Ibid.

demand from ourselves and from our life-pursuits that they feel in accordance with that joy which we know ourselves to be capable of.[18]

It is because the erotic may be expressed in myriad places that Lorde is critiquing the ways *men have misused the erotic against women* as "actresses" in pornographic print and film. Porn is false feeling. She understands that this erotic sensibility often occurs in the bedroom, but ultimately what Lorde is trying to promote is for women to begin to make themselves aware of their true erotic capacity.

This is especially important coming from Lorde, a self-identified lesbian for whom sexual expression through intimate, erotic sex was clearly a fact of her life. Any discussion of the erotic is strengthened by a courageous discussion about sexual expression. Is such discussion only permitted in the realm of fictitious and pornographic writing? If so, doesn't that *ipso facto* make Lorde's point?

This is why works like Brown's and Copeland's ought not to be the only works available to Black LGBTQ persons and our allies. We need extensive and frank discussion about the loving ways in which LGBTQ sexuality is expressed, as well as reflection on God's gracious act of creating our bodies in God's image and likeness. I admit I am imposing my own passion for an outright activism against homophobic church teaching. Because Copeland does such a fine job in chapter three of articulating Catholic Church teaching and specifically how the Church's teaching is oppressive to LGBTQ persons, she has certainly given queer womanists a rich theological resource to develop helpful resistance methods. Likewise Brown's work, with her exceptional understanding of Black church culture and stance against Black homophobia, has helped to shift our discussions of the impact of corrupt teaching about sexuality on our black bodies.

The bodies of Black LBTQ women are part of the body of Jesus Christ[19] who, according to Copeland, "embraces *all* our bodies passionately, revalorizes them as embodied mystery, and reorients sexual desire toward God's desire for us in and through our sexuality."[20] This is no puritanical argument. It is inclusive and affirming of Black LBTQ women and reminds the church of the queer nature of Christ's body.

18. Ibid., 57.
19. Ibid., 78.
20. Ibid., 80.

Moreover, we need more Black theologians willing to say categorically, "Human sexuality as expressed through consensual loving actions including intercourse is not sin." LGBTQ persons should ignore Church teaching against consensual sex as an expression of love between same-sex persons. They should derive every possible pleasure from engaging in it and understand it as a healthy expression of what it means to be human. Without this affirmation and scholarly assessment of impractical and poor church theology, we have few resources that will help us be whole persons within the churches we adore.

It falls to Queer womanist theologians to demonstrate a healthy perspective on sexuality that is not silent on the subject of sex acts (including intercourse) and on the power of the erotic, the sensual. We must speak of the healthy expression of sexuality in ways that do not limit Black queer persons or require that we hand over our sexual drives and expression to be subsumed by the Church's demands that we be good celibate Christian queers.

In chapter seven, I offer an analysis of *imago Dei* that speaks concretely to LGBTQ sexuality. I do so not for the purpose of empty sex-talk but to exemplify a way to discuss sex acts that neither dismisses the work of God in our lives nor engages sex only as juicy rhetoric.

The lived experiences of Black LBTQ women is of utmost importance though our inclusion in womanist scholarship has been dismally low. Some Black scholars like Cheryl Sanders, pastor of 3rd St. Church of God and professor at Howard University School of Divinity, both in Washington, D.C. have argued the term "womanist" may not be helpful for the Black community because part of its definition, "women who love other women sexually" conveys a moral perspective that is not helpful to the Black church or community.

> In my view there is a fundamental discrepancy between the womanist criteria would affirm and/or advocate homosexual practice, and the ethical norms the black church might employ to promote the survival and wholeness of black families. It is problematic for those of us who claim connectedness to and concern for those two institutions . . . There is a great need for the black churches to promote a positive sexual ethics within the black community as one means of responding to the growing normalization of the single-parent family, and the attendant increases in poverty, welfare dependency, and a host of other problems . . . The womanist nomenclature, however, conveys a sexual ethics that is ambivalent

at best with respect to the value of heterosexual monogamy within the black community.[21]

We are over two decades removed from the time of this essay and two things remain the same: Dr. Sanders' perspective and the presence of Black LBTQ women in black churches and communities. Moreover all have survived and some strive in the wake of federal laws enacted in support of same-sex marriage. There is no evidence that Christian moral reasoning that affirms the lives of LGBTQ persons impedes or devalues heterosexual monogamy, black families or the ministry of the black churches to respond to the socio-political issues Dr. Sanders raised. Most importantly, the most deficient element of Sanders' essay is that it does not explore the works of womanist scholars. According to M. Shawn Copeland, "Notably absent from her analysis are quotations from works by those scholars who use womanist to describe their work. Their voices are silent. Without their words, it is not possible to determine the accuracy of Sanders' understanding, interpretation, and judgment of their work. It is not possible to judge her evaluation of their claims and proposals in any specific way.[22]

Though the absence of womanist voices in Sanders' essay critical of homosexuality was detrimental to her analysis even more telling was the minimal research by womanist scholars on the lives of Black lesbian, bisexual and transgender women. Rene Hill in her essay, "Who Are We For Each Other? Sexism, Sexuality, and Womanist Theology" critiqued this silence in womanist scholarship saying,

> Christian womanists have failed to recognise [sic] heterosexism and homophobia as points of oppression that need to be resisted if all Black women (straight, lesbian and bisexual) are to have liberation and a sense of their own power. Some womanists have avoided the issues of sexuality and sexual orientation by being selective in the parts of Walker's definition of womanism. This tendency to be selective implies that it is possible to be selective about who deserves liberation and visibility. If Black Christian theologians are going to appropriate Walker's definition of womanism, relationships between women, including lesbianism, must be addressed.[23]

21. Sanders, "Roundtable Discussion: Christian Ethics and Theology in Womanist Perspective," 83–112.

22. Ibid.

23 Hill, "Who Are We For Each Other? Sexism, Sexuality, and Womanist Theology," 345–51.

A lot of ground has been covered since these early debates. The Womanist Approaches to Religion and Society Group of AAR has explored the struggles of Black LBTQ women during several of its sessions and I, an out queer lesbian womanist am co-chair of the group. Womanist scholars like Monica Coleman, Nikki Young and Elonda Clay are using an intersectional analysis using Black LBTQ women's experience as a source for doing theology.

It would, nevertheless, be incorrect to suggest the only concern of womanist theology is Black women and Black culture. We are interested in exposing discrimination of Black women in particular and women in general. We are concerned about Black communities in particular but Creation in general. Nowadays our work is expansive addressing ecological needs, the struggle for quality education, self-care, quality of care for the poor and oppressed, and so forth.

Queer womanist scholars employ the label womanist because it suits our existential situation and research passions. As queers we assert our right to name our own sexual identities and to use our experiences as Black queer womanists as influential to our critical reflections about Black women, the Black community, and Creation. As persons of faith, we "love the Spirit" and seek to call attention to the myriad ways Black queer women honor the Divine. Though this work is written from a Christian context, Black queer womanists are from many faith traditions. In queer womanist methodology we investigate those points of departure integral to womanist theology: race, sex, class and gender.

Yet we are also aware of the inherent problems of calling ourselves womanists with an added descriptor, queer. Some might argue that appropriating "queer" is tacit acceptance of a term that has been hurled at LGBTQ persons by bigots for many years. It is a constant reminder of the pain inflicted by vociferous critics expressing callous disregard for the struggle for human rights. Others may argue that womanist is but another category serving the hegemonic heterosexual social construct, a term that threatens to erase the plight of Black queer persons who do not self-identify with the gender expressions woman or man.

These are all valid concerns. Language is a powerful resource and we must always consider how it influences and is influenced by our social locations. Though we may debate the viability of LGBTQ lexicons internal community expressions, the term womanist has not yet risen to the level of awareness among Black LGBTQ persons or the larger community so as to make an indubitable label. Black LBTQ must guard against linguistic representations that perpetuate binaries or naively endorse a kind of internalized oppression. Taking a bit of editorial liberty, the most pressing question on this matter is one expressed by Dr. Katie Cannon: "Does the term *womanist* provide an appropriate frame of reference for the ethical and theological statements now being generated by black [LBTQ] women?"[24]

For these reasons, it is important to explain the history and meaning of queer theology and show how it may or may not be useful in Black culture.

24. Ibid. Bracketed language mine.

CHAPTER 2

Philosophical Background
to Queer Theology

FEMINIST SCHOLARS, SUCH AS Teresa de Lauretis, Judith Butler, and Eve Kosofsky Sedgwick, but also twentieth-century French post-structuralism significantly influenced the early work of queer activists and queer theorists.[1] Great philosophers such as Jacques Derrida and Michel Foucault, who used the method now known as deconstruction, were important to the rise of post-structuralism in literary analysis. This school of thought is so embedded in queer theory (and theology) that I have come to think of it somewhat as Gary Busey says of acting, "Acting is the absence of acting."[2] To do it well, *to queer*, is simply to do it, without drawing attention to the mechanics, though they are operative in every work. In this way, though many queer theologians cover the history of the term "queer" (especially the gay rights movement), they "just do it," just go about the business of postulating *queer* without helping the novice understand the fundamental methodology that makes up the grounds of their arguments. One gets to the "queering" as though it were *a priori* knowledge.

While this may be good for acting, it is frustrating to the novice reader. To understand queer works you really need some "in-road" into the dialogue. I am not suggesting that every work needs to function as a primer. One learns the basics and then progresses to more challenging works. My concern is to help persons who want to be involved in this discourse

---

1. The lesbian and gay movements taking place in the United States and around the world influenced many queer theorists, including the ones I have mentioned.

2. Gary Busey, *All-Star Celebrity Apprentice*, 2013, Episode 9.

understand some of its basic suppositions and why those suppositions are important. So rather than moving forward having given–in the introductory chapter—only some of the history of the term itself, what follows is a rather cursory, but I hope helpful, introduction to one of the key critical approaches from which queer theory is derived: deconstruction. Like building blocks, the student of queer theology should spend some time reviewing deconstruction, which is foundational to understanding the philosophical arguments that went before and into queer theory and queer theology.

Now granted this project cannot sufficiently cover all these approaches in any way other than to give the reader a modest and cursory glimpse of major literary and philosophical approaches. But I am convinced that that is enough to help uncover some rationale for where we are in the field of queer theology. There would be no queer theology without the very rich deconstructive work done by poststructuralists themselves borrowing and critiquing philosophical work from the several eras discussed in the following summary.

I am also very interested as an African American to look into the impact of the civil rights movement on the lives of two of its strongest leaders whose self-identities as a gay man and as a man trapped in a woman's body were made subservient or denigrated for the sake of mobilizing efforts around "Blackness" as a politicized identity. Womanist queer theology must investigate how the practice of identity politics has done and continues to do damage to women and Black communities. Our methodological concerns should include a sound critique of essentialism within our communities and avoidance when possible within our writing.[3] It makes no sense to have a theoretical framework that purports to take seriously "the people" if we intentionally or unintentionally exclude and therefore marginalize other persons. For Black LBTQ women, this means that I am making the case that no one of our self-identities is subordinate or should be made subordinate to the other. Of course, I am writing with the benefit of history—of knowing that often Black women and Black LBTQ women have placed or been made to place their own self-interests on the backburner for the purported sake of the uplift of the race. This is a matter I will tie into this discussion of the philosophical underpinnings of queer theology particularly given my womanist perspective of queer theology.

---

3. Admittedly, there are times when I have used language such as "the Black Church," "Black people," etc., to make fairly general but poignant points. I am not sure that we writers will do away with such generalizations, but I am working on it.

The Philosophical Foundations of Queer Theology

The age that followed the European Enlightenment era (also known as the Age of Reason[4]), that of *modernity*, is characterized by the shift from "unquestionable" knowledge and the near idealization of science to more critical reflections about life and especially about what was presented as "truth." With modernity came a marked skepticism about empirical methodology, which upheld scientific observation as the only reliable means of acquiring knowledge.

Particularly with Immanuel Kant,[5] thinkers of this era argued that science was limited in its ability to provide knowledge. Knowledge is neither based solely on empiricism nor on rationalism. Kant argued for a synthesis of both as can be seen in his work, *Critique of Pure Reason*. Kant posited that science is only capable of helping humans obtain knowledge of "appearances" that make up our experiences (phenomena) and not the "thing itself" (*noumena*). The *noumenon* exists outside our experience. Humans cannot experience it as *noumena* are of another dimension/reality.[6]

This is not to say that Kant was against objective knowledge. I read Kant as saying that humans as rational beings could discover truth, but that our understanding (reason) was limited/constrained regarding what truth we can experience. We know phenomena (that which we experience) but not reality itself; we cannot know the "thing itself," the noumenon. Therefore, the act of "knowing" happens as an activity of the mind of the self-differentiated self in relationship to the world (a phenomenon that we can experience). There is an objective validity of the phenomena, a truth to our experiences. Queer theory writings that use experience as one of its sources reflect this way of thinking. For example, Judith Butler's experiences within the context of a lesbian and gay community on the east coast of the United

---

4. Understood as the era in which reason and science replaced religion as the doorway to knowledge and thereby human progress. Here I am thinking of intellectual philosophers such as Kant, Descartes, Spinoza, and Locke.

5. I am aware of Kant's racism and that his theories and vile comments regarding race, especially of Africans and Negroes, helped shape race theories during the Enlightenment era and now. Though the denunciation of slavery can be found in his writings (e.g., *Toward Perpetual Peace*), I have found no evidence to suggest his denunciation of slavery was followed by an admission that the African or the "Negro" was equal to what he would call the "white race." I include Kant in this work because of the impact his work had on Enlightenment philosophy and its historical place in Queer Theory.

6. Kant, *Critique of Pure Reason*.

States is "one aspect of the conditions" of production in her now-classic book, *Gender Trouble*.[7]

Rather than focusing on objectivity and the evolution of the mind as did Kant and others, *postmodern* literary and philosophical theorists are concerned with language and especially semiotic analysis. They examine signs (here, we look especially at linguistic signs), convinced that signs give meaning and are the expression of thought. Particularly with literature, philosophers argued that the idea of objectivity was elusive because of the multiple interpretations of the text. Against the Enlightenment era perspective that presumed knowledge could be purely objective–that is, unbiased and factual–thinkers of our time assert a rather epistemological skepticism. They scoff at the idea of objective, uninfluenced knowledge or the unity of the human subject. Their scholarship pays attention to the capacity of the individual to do critical self-reflection. And so attention to atomistic, individualism has flourished.

Structuralism, an intellectual movement that includes a range of theoretical perspectives. It is a consideration of the universal done by analyzing the building blocks of smaller relationships that support the universal. The analysis does not to pull out meaning from the text but considers the ways in which structures of meaning are pulled from the text. It was held to be an objective and deep inquiry into the larger phenomena, rather than into individual subjects. Structuralism, with regards to literature, emphasized understanding the structural order that exists within every text as a means of understanding the larger text.

One of the most common terms used in queer theory results from the work of Swiss linguist Ferdinand de Saussure, who understood language as "a social institution . . . a system of signs that express ideas."[8] Saussure created *semiology*, "the science that studies the life of signs within society" and felt that it should fall under the discipline of social psychology.[9] The sign is foundational to language and consists of both the letters of words and the meaning that combined letters (the signified) hold. Saussure stated, "By studying rites, customs, etc. as signs, I believe that we shall throw new light on the facts and point up the need for including them in a science of semiology and explaining them by its laws."[10]

7. Butler, *Gender Trouble: Feminism and the Subversion of Identity*, xvii.

8. Saussure, *Course in General Linguistics*, 73–74.

9. Ibid.

10. Ibid., 76.

Having placed the study of speech under the rubric of social psychology, he insisted that semiotics not be understood to be the same as linguistics, "whose sole object is language."[11] It was the linguistics of language that captured Saussure's interest, particularly the rules with which the system of signs functioned. "The culture of a nation exerts its influence on its language, and the language, on the other hand, is largely responsible for the nation."[12] This exertion of cultural influence on language is an important argument in queer theory and queer theology. They will argue that there is no neutrality in language and what is more, that language has been used to oppress LGBTQ persons.

One of the most important concepts in queer theory is often credited to Saussure's notion of *binary opposition*. On this topic, University of Toronto professor emeritus Mario Valdés, whose research areas include the theory of literature wrote:

> In a binary opposition the two poles must not only be opposed to each other but must also be in exclusive opposition to each other; in other words, they are bound in polar opposition like the positive and negative charge of an electrical current . . . Structural linguistics, which defines language as a system of functional relations, presupposes binary oppositions of the phonological elements of language as the basis and model of its analysis.[13]

Saussure gave prominence to this theory in his work and felt strongly that "language is a system of differences in which all elements are defined solely by their relations with one another."[14] Nowadays we carry on about the problem of binary categories without so much as a nod to thinkers like Saussure.

Similarly, in the work of most queer theorists one often sees the critique of *dichotomies* articulated, again drawing upon Saussurean theory. These theorists are often critical of the use of rigid categories, especially the cultural use of binary categories such as male/female, feminine/masculine. Particularly related to gender identity, queer theorists reject the notion that gender can be construed in such limited fashion.

Buttressed by the work of Algerian-French philosopher Jacques Derrida, queer theorists will often apply a method known as *deconstruction*.

11. Ibid., 78.

12. Ibid., 79.

13. Valdés, "Binary Opposition," 511.

14. Culler, *Ferdinand de Saussure*,.

Derrida was critical of the theory of binary opposites, and argued that their use was a matter of manipulation (power).

> One particular kind of deconstruction is a critique of binary op-
> positions. According to Derrida, there are many such oppositions
> in Western thought: for example life/death, presence/absence
> and so on. Derrida says that in each opposition one of the pair
> is privileged over the other. The privileged one is the one most
> associated with the phallus or else with the *logos* (which is what
> he called speech-thought). However, the other one of the pair is
> always essential to the first: without death there is no life, and so
> on. Deconstruction aims to unpack the historical power imbal-
> ances in these oppositions by examining the importance within
> the text of the subsidiary half of each opposition.[15]

Deconstructing the text to expose its contradictions and the impossibility of a unified and precise interpretation became the work of philosophical and literary postmodernists. As a literary strategy, deconstruction is the unpacking, the deep examination of textual layers of meaning. One is try-ing to uncover from within the text how it compliments, contradicts, and unfolds. Derrida contended that deconstruction was merely a name for the self- or auto- deconstruction of certain philosophical and literary texts, whose projects at unity or comprehension ultimately defeat themselves from within.

Not only were texts "unpacked" but so also were the various elements of our human living. This exposition should not be understood as a brutal stripping of texts but as an appreciative examination of texts as one is reflec-tively "within" the text. Deconstructionists argue for multiple meanings in the text and reality and therefore for the inability to get at a literal meaning of the text and at a pure objective knowledge. They assert the impossibil-ity of a universal "knowing" and in their work seek to show that what is "known" is limited because it is gained through a hermeneutic informed by the context of the observer.

Meaning then, as construed within the text, is never fixed. Therefore what we understand as a fixed reality is questionable since will be uncov-ered in the analysis of the language of a given culture will be hidden and demonstrate multiple meanings of any given context. Even knowledge, and epistemology (how we know what we know) is a matter of interpretation. Therefore, poststructuralists critique poststructuralism with its emphasis

15. Ruso, "Jacques Derrida and Deconstruction."

on understanding patterns or structures within a unique system (or text) that shows its relationship to a larger system of signs as being static and ignoring the impact of context. The idea of exploring the phenomena of how meaning is created rather than attending to determining the actual meaning of a particular text or reality was an approach that was difficult to understand. As an approach, structural exegesis sought to interpret the text not by attention to its historical elements but to its linguistic ones, deriving structures of meaning from the language of the scriptures.

As a reaction to structuralism, poststructuralists such as Michele Foucault began to take seriously the enterprise of knowledge and its relationship to power (though he would not like this labeling). In his work on sexuality he argued that knowledge is controlled by power. It does this through discourse. Take for instance how he describes power's relationship to discourse in order to control sex: "power acts by laying down the rule: power's hold on sex is maintained through language, or rather through the act of discourse that creates, from the very fact that it is articulated, a rule of law. It speaks, and that is the rule."[16]

Filtering data through the context (to include experience and culture) of the observer means—according to poststructuralist philosophers—that there is no disinterested, unbiased, or objective knowledge as purported by structuralists. However, this presents a problem. If texts, institutions, etc. have no definable meanings and if all knowledge is biased, what then are we to think of the concrete, material nature of our lives? If my experience of life influences my understanding of reality, is all knowledge therefore relative and subjective? Is everything up for grabs? The primary critique of poststructuralist thought then is this question: If truth is unknowable, how do we know it is unknowable? That is, if there is no absolute truth, then the theory that there is no absolute truth is inherently contradictory and should not be believed absolutely. The problem is presented as somewhat of an ultimatum: Either there is an ultimate truth or not. Put this way, one has to wonder if it is possible to reach a détente on the matter, especially with regards to social categories.

This is where we turn to what is being called *identity politics* because it is such a dominant theme in today's discussion of theologies of liberation. The argument of postmodernism is that experiences are so differentiated that no one person can speak authoritatively for any one group. Identities such as race or gender are social constructions and there exists no one

16. Foucault, *History of Sexuality*, 83.

archetypal experience, no single biological reality that speaks for an entire body of people. For instance, the so-called leaders of identity-based liberation movements are critiqued (and rightly so) because they often point to group ideals using flawed commonalities. As much as I respect and admire Rev. Al Sharpton for the excellent work he has done on equal rights of all people, more than a few Black persons defiantly declare, "He doesn't speak for me. He's just an opportunist!" The underlying basis of their argument— which is much larger than the object of their protest—is racial categories, in this case the Black race, is a specious notion. Are there clear and verifiable epistemological traits that can be used to identify blackness as a race or culture? Or are these merely social constructions based on experience and phenotypes?

It is the postmodernist skepticism of identities that I think both drives and divides the conversation. Put it like this: Is there a way in which Rev. Sharpton or any one person can "speak for Black people"? Is there an ultimate truth about what it means to be Black? As an identity, there really is no monolithic, all essentially like-minded community or group of persons that we can categorize as "Black people." We can also say, as ultimate truth, "The Black church as one entity does not exist." Therefore when we speak of "Black people" and "the Black Church" we are speaking of subjective constructs.

This is a driving and powerful perspective of the point to be made about the subjectivity of identity categories. What divides the conversation is the critical debate about our cultural experiences as identified by categories of race, gender, sexuality, etc. To wit, the subjective category of *lesbian* impacts my cultural experiences to the extent that I understand myself to be *lesbian*. Yet while my identity as a *lesbian* is real to me only if I understand myself to be *lesbian*, the impact of that category on my life is not solely dictated by my self-identity. There are countless numbers of persons who have been bullied because they were perceived as lesbian or gay; countless numbers of persons who were ostracized from one racial culture because their self-identity was not consistent with a particular phenotype and racial category.

What postmodernism has given us is indeed a way to speak of the social construction of our realities and especially the social construction of the categories of our existence whether by race, gender, class, etc. Those categories are certainly subjective. However, the language of these categories, the words which signify how we are perceived in society, do objectively impact our social location. Therefore marginalized persons do well to develop modes of describing the experiential consequences of these categories.

When I write, as a self-identified African American queer lesbian woman, I am writing based upon my context and the common and even unique experiences of my embodied self in contrast to the experiences of other lesbian women in particular and human beings in general. I believe it to be a legitimate academic endeavor to inquire whether there may be some verifiable common sets of experiences pressing upon the lives of LGBTQ persons specifically because of their self-identity. And yet I bemoan the fact of experiences that have been and are so negatively discriminatory in nature.

The chief question becomes whether because of their experiences based on identity categories there is also the possibility that there is a way of "knowing" the world from the perspective of persons who self-identify with these various categories. For instance, historically racial identity has been used to determine the social location of Black people in our nation. The constructed racial identities have had economic and political consequences in our society because persons placed within these categories have been made to live under the constraints of these constructs building the industries of our nation and challenging the politics of our nation.

To challenge constructions of identity as discriminatory, persons have come together and built coalitions of solidarity to challenge stereotypes and prejudices. They have often deconstructed the categories in order to call into question the attending prejudices built into our culture and politics and to show what harm is done when persons are placed into categories that marginalize and oppress.

Shifting just a bit, let's me illustrate some of the claims I have made in this discourse on the contributions of French philosophers to queer theory to get a better understanding of some of the dynamics at work during the civil rights movement.

Understanding the Impact of Race as a Socially Constructed Category to the Civil Rights Movement

Gathering knowledge about the causal impact of race on social location was critical to the civil rights movement of the 1960s. It is very important to note that postmodernism emerged during this era, a time which emphasized freedom and a growing respect for differences. Using identity to articulate respect for human freedom was part of the driving force of the civil rights movement. I remember the very powerful sign carried by Black men: "I Am A Man." It touched the hearts of many Black men and women and is a notable placard being carried in today's protests being held in Ferguson, Mo. It said what most had experienced: Of being called "boy," of being discriminated against on the basis of race constructs, of the insistence of protecting their dignity, and of being valued only as of servants to white men and women.

What is important to remember of that time is that the category "man" was not an acceptable designation for persons of African descent. Here is an example of a socially constructed category that was largely assumed to be attributable only to men of European descent whose phenotype carried the label "white." Black men demanded that the category, and specifically the respect that came with the category, be afforded them as American citizens. Black people—as a unified self-identified group—through the representation of lawyers such as Thurgood Marshall, were able to have several cases for equal rights taken all the way to the Supreme Court, including Brown vs. The Board of Education of Topeka.[17] The Civil Rights Act of 1964 outlawed race discrimination and granted Black persons the equal recognitions and protections of the federal law. It also addressed other designations such as color, religion, and sex.

Without such designations we could not speak of a "protected class" of characteristics such as race, class, religion, sex, or age in much of our anti-discrimination laws. So, again, while the categories are subjective, our history has shown that not only is identity as real as an individual perceives it to be, the impact is as real as the society in which we live perceives it to be. The constructs can be experienced as lived reality despite the subjectivity of the constructs. And while no one person can speak for an entire body of people, there are many occasions when for the sake of justice we need to address discrimination and do so on the basis of solidarity, where both discrimination and solidarity are articulated by the language of categories. Indeed: *sticks and stones may break your bones and yes, being perceived in a particular category can also hurt you.*

Indicative of my argument is the work of SCLC chief of staff, Ella Baker, one of the principal organizers of the student sit-ins. She understood perhaps more than any of the leaders of that time that what plagued Black

17. See Goldman and Gallen, *Thurgood Marshall, Justice for All.*

people was not only a matter of individual freedoms or of individual recognition but also of how we perceive each other as human beings without
categories. In what is now known as the Shaw Conference "Bigger Than
a Hamburger" speech, Baker argued that, "the movement was concerned
with the moral implications of racial discrimination for the 'whole world'
and the 'Human Race.'"[18]

Tragically, Ms. Baker also had to bear the brunt of discrimination
within the same oppressed community for which she worked so diligently.
Black men who carried signs demanding recognition and respect as citizens of this country were at the same time seeking to deny Ms. Baker of
any status as a leader in the movement solely on the basis of her gender.
Through an informal intersectional analysis, she was able to understand
the weakness of the socially constructed system of the 1960s civil rights
campaign that was undergirded by a dynamic of gender stratification that
required women be subordinate to men. Thus, Ms. Baker often spoke of
"participatory democracy" which was both her criticism of the dominant
male leadership structure of the NAACP and of the facts that its leadership
was composed largely of clergy. Her vision was one of full inclusion: of clergy and laity, students and professionals, young and old, men and women.

Ms. Baker was a close ally of Bayard Rustin, the Black Quaker activist
to whom we owe a debt of gratitude for his role in bringing the March on
Washington to fruition. As a classic textbook study of intersectional oppression, Rustin's life as a Black male civil rights leader cannot be thoroughly appreciated without knowing that because he was gay, many of the
Black male clergy considered him a liability. Both categories, Black and gay,
impacted his social location and shaped his life.

What I find fascinating is the incredibly important work to which
these two activists committed themselves at the same time as enduring multiple forms of discrimination from several sides. Their genius made them
a formidable team. Though Rustin was problematic to some feminists,[19] he
had an ally in Baker. According to historian and political activist Barbara
Ransby,

18. Baker, "Bigger Than a Hamburger."

19. Pauli Murray wrote to Rustin on August 12, 1971, to submit her resignation from
the Executive Board of the A. Philip Randolph Institute. She asked this question: "How
does it happen that of an Executive Board of 41, only two are women—Eleanor Holmes
Norton and myself—both of whom are feminists and whose names have some public
exchange value but who do not stand for the implicitly male-dominated nature of the
Institute?" Schlesinger Library, Radcliff Institute, Harvard University, 1898, 106.

Ella Baker knew Rustin was gay and seemingly accepted him without condition, later reflecting that his homosexuality may have been one of the reasons that he opted to keep a low profile during his long, active political career in a wide range of organizations and campaigns . . . Baker, Levison, and Rustin were an unlikely threesome in many respects, but their ideas and political passions drew them together and enabled them to become comrades and friends.[20]

Both Rustin and Baker shared ideas about the inherent rights and freedoms of each human being and understood the effects of power. Rustin countered the political order in Washington; Baker countered both that order and the hierarchy of the NAACP. In a very pragmatic philosophical sense the civil rights movement used discourse as a tool of attack and defense in order to shift the power relation for the benefit of producing a reality more just for Black citizens. Like Foucault, both Baker and Rustin understood that power is engendered by knowledge. Both aimed at dismantling the American cultural perception of Black persons that had been constructed upon stereotypical knowledge. Therefore, the methodology they (and many others) used was a far-reaching education of Black persons that intended to improve and uplift the "consciousness of a people."

This uplift included a deconstruction of racial categories, to include the term *Negro*. In its place came the terms *Black*, *Afro-American* and *African American*. "Say it loud. I'm Black and I'm proud!" became the mantra within many communities of predominantly persons of African descent. Admittedly, this was yet another construction of group identity, yet more essentialist categories. Nonetheless, at the time this approach to "uniting the people" was a healing balm, a social phenomenon of the oppressed exercising a sense of power and agency never before believed possible. It was the rejection of the negative stereotype and the transformation of one's own sense of identity through positive consciousness-raising, at times even reclaiming identities thought to be pejorative (as is the case with the term *queer*).

Identity categories are therefore very complex. Using a deconstructive strategy helps queer theorists and scholars to show the heterogeneity, historical context, arbitrariness, unverifiable essentialism of identity categories and even their capacity to be deployed as mechanisms of solidarity, liberation, and oppression. The deconstructive critique of categories brought to

20. Ransby, *Ella Baker and the Black Freedom Movement*, 163–64.

bear within Queer Theology is useful in that it helps scholars analyze the biblical text by deconstructing readings of sacred scripture in order to allow for alternative interpretations. It specifically addresses the complexities of gender identities in the Bible and in our world. And it demonstrates over and over again that gender is rendered by performance, that there is no unique and essential way of being man or woman, heterosexual, homosexual, bisexual, or transgender. There exists no objective, epistemological, and monolithic construct for sexual identities. They are simply too vast, too complex, and too fluid.

Queering, as a theological methodology, is a deconstruction and re-evaluation of gender perspectives that uses as its framework queer theory and as its resources scripture, reason, tradition, and experience. Some have seen its challenge to heteronormativity as a challenge to the Church universal. However, queer theologians must be comfortable with the Church being challenged. We come from a long history of the Church's doctrine and dogma being challenged. It has become better and its theology much healthier when it must explores its conceptualizations of Christ as its head and the people who are its members. Queer theology is the Church's pièce de résistance of the twenty-first century in that if offers an opportunity to include rather than exclude more voices within our various communities.

CHAPTER 3

Enable Queer-y

THE TERM "QUEER" WAS originally meant to describe any person considered "strange," and it is still used in this way today. But the term at one time was also an acceptably used form of self-identification by gay men. It functioned as a linguistic designation to describe the social stratification that existed within the gay subculture. Indeed, professor of history George Chauncey in his examination of New York prior to World War II distinguishes between several sectors of gay male life. The more "masculine" gendered gay men self-identified as *queer*. "Earlier terms–*fairy*, *queer* and *trade* most commonly–had distinguished various types of homosexually active men: effeminate homosexuals, more conventional homosexuals, and masculine heterosexuals who would accept homosexual advances, to use today's nomenclature."[1]

To the queer of those days it was one thing to be considered "different," quite another to be thought flamboyant with one's difference. According to Chauncey, gay men in the early twentieth century who wanted to present a more masculine gender performance preferred to be called *queer*. During those prewar years, "queer did not presume that the men it denoted were effeminate, for many queers were repelled by the style of the fairy and his loss of manly status, and almost all were careful to distinguish themselves from such men."[2]

Chauncey also argues that this actually designated something deeper than behavior or performativity, and that the distinctions between *fairies*

1. Chauncey, *Gay New York*, 20.
2. Ibid., 16.

and *queers* were also related to class. The fairies were of the working-class while queers were of the middle-class communities.[3] Thus, it was also social stratification that affected the self-image of gay men, and no doubt of the entire LGBTQ community.

The outstanding advances made by Blacks in the literary, music, and art worlds during what is now called the Harlem Renaissance also mark this time period. Not only artistically, the Harlem Renaissance was a time of "coming out for Black gays and lesbians. Historians Juan Battle and Natalie Bennett describe this vibrant subculture in the Black community:

> Homoerotic socializing was a major feature of Harlem life in the 1920s and 1930s. It was also the setting for rent parties and buffet flats–all-night events for gay, lesbian, bisexual, and sexually adventurous persons that were held in private homes and featured food, drink, gambling, sex, and/or any combination thereof. Gay male and lesbian revues and cabarets were also frequent, as were drag balls–what Langston Hughes called "Spectacles in Color"–which were attended by large numbers of Black gay men and lesbians, where both men and women could dress as they desired and dance with whomever they pleased.[4]

The early twentieth century, especially prewar years, "permitted" both discreet and open sexual exploration and participation for *queers* and *fairies*, white gay men and lesbians, as well as for persons of color. In a subculture considered relatively small and certainly not with a large pool of available *trades*, the more "conventional homosexuals" (to use Chauncey's phrase) did not want to be classified as *flaming* fairies. But this began to change by the middle of the century. By the 1950s,

> Younger men rejected *queer* as a pejorative name that others had given them, which highlighted their difference from other men. Even though many 'queers' had also rejected the effeminacy of the fairies, younger men were well aware that in the eyes of straight men their 'queerness' hinged on their supposed gender deviance.[5]

The tide had turned. The degree to which *queer* had been acceptable self-identifying language began to diminish. By the 1950s the nation had gone through the Great Depression and World War II, and public policy against gay and lesbian persons increased significantly. To be *queer* was to

3. Ibid.

4. Battle and Bennett, "Striving for Place," 416–17.

5. Chauncey, *Gay New York*, 19.

be a sexually recalcitrant and abhorrent individual, something from which younger gays were determined to distance themselves Nonetheless, the term *queer* was not totally dismissed. "Some men, especially older ones . . . continued to prefer *queer* to *gay*, in part because of gay's initial association with the fairies."[6]

From its early reference as a mechanism of shame through the early gay liberation era to the setting of post-structural investigations about language and power, the term remained part of the gay lexicon and has now been rather thoroughly reclaimed from its pejorative use. What is more, it has transcended the gay community and is used to refer to any number of groups who take issue with the idea that one's sexuality is fixed and only acceptable within the binary realm of male/female. While we may debate whether it should be used at all and who or what group may use it, *queer*, like *nigger*, is now part of the *langue de la journée*.

The fact that queer is now a politically acceptable term is due to the rigorous work of LGBT activists against political and police oppression. Organizations such as the Homophile Movement, the Mattachine Society, and Daughters of Bilitis; events like the *One, Inc.* vs. Olesen case which affirmed the LGBT magazine's first amendment right,[7] the 1969 Stonewall Riots, the release of the Kinsey Report, and the 1970 Christopher St. Liberation Day (which would become Gay Pride Day)[8] are all part of the successful moments of the LGBTQ revolution.

Alongside the events of the gay rights revolution was the academic work of theorists such Michel Foucault whose work influenced aforementioned feminist and lesbian scholars such as Teresa de Lauretis, Judith Butler, and Eve Sedgwick. In his groundbreaking work, *History of Sexuality*, Foucault reviewed the ways in which sexuality was perceived and discussed. Rather than agreeing with the "repressive hypothesis,, that is, that our discussions of sex have been repressed, Foucault argues that not only has sex been discussed but it has also become an object of knowledge.[9] As a philosopher and historian, Foucault sees the connections between discourse, knowledge, and power. The powerful bourgeoisie class controls discourse, controls what can be said of sex, and thus controls knowledge about sex. However, the attempt to control discourse about sex only led to

6. Ibid., 19.

7. PBS.org, "Timeline: Milestones in the American Gay Rights Movement."

8. Ibid.

9. Foucault, *History of Sexuality*, 54.

more discourse about sex and ultimately to homosexuality being seen not as an act but as an identity. Homosexuality as an identity was soon to be scrutinized by medical, psychological, and ministerial powers.

> This new persecution of the peripheral sexualities entailed an *incorporation of perversions* and a new *specification of individuals* . . . The nineteenth-century homosexual became a personage, a past, a case history, and a childhood, in addition to being a type of life, a life form, and a morphology, with an indiscreet anatomy and possibly a mysterious physiology. Nothing that went into his total composition was unaffected by his sexuality.[10]

It is precisely because homosexuality continues to be identified with personhood, indeed because those who have taken it upon themselves to self-identify as lesbian, gay, bisexual, and transgender, that my explication of Black queer theology is not wholly constituted upon the largely poststructural skepticism of identity and experiential knowledge. In this twenty-first century sexual identity matters and those who self-identify with any of the societal markers of *homosexual* run the risk of persecution, no matter that the term queer has become more socially acceptable and no matter that our country has enacted many laws to ensure our civil rights. To many people, we are still *perverts*. To many, the Black pervert is the most dangerous threat to the American ideal. Because the Black conservative bourgeoisie has joined the attack on our personhood, Black LGBTQ persons cannot allow the discourse to be controlled such that our existence within the Black community is denied or made invisible. Like Foucault, we understand the connection between discourse, knowledge, and power. However, we cannot easily dismiss categories only as social constructs of reality.

Here, the work of postpositivist realism scholar Paula Moya and Chicana feminist Cherríe Moraga informs my work. These authors argue that the reclaiming of identities is important for the following reasons:

> Cultural identities are not only and always 'wounded attachments.' They can also be enabling, enlightening, and enriching structures of attachment and feeling . . . The significance of identity depends partly on the fact that goods and resources are still distributed according to identity categories . . . Who we are . . . will significantly affect our life chances: where we can live, whom we will marry (or where we can marry), and what kinds of educational and employment opportunities will be available to us . . . an ability to take

10. Ibid., 42.

effective steps toward progressive social change is predicated on
an acknowledgment of, and a familiarity with, past and present
structures of inequality–structures that are often highly correlated
with categories of identity . . . Finally, we have undertaken the task
of reclaiming identity because 'identities' are evaluatable theoretical claims that have epistemic consequences.[11]

Because identities matter much within the cultures of persons of
color, I emphasize the cultural dynamics of being both Black and queer
while at the same time being concerned with the essentialism and who gets
to define the characteristics of what it means to be Black and/or queer. To
address the discursive and performative nature of gender should not also
mean that we lose or set aside our cultural identities.

Black LGBTQ identified persons must be quite cautious when it
comes to the term *queer* if that naming includes a rejection of our ability to
claim as objective our knowledge of our own sexual identity, which is often
mediated by our experiences in the world and in our culture. Rather than
quibble over the impact of language on the construction of identity, queer
persons of color live, day in and day out, with the impact of identity. We
can ill afford to participate in deconstructing gender in the ways contemporary white queers have often advocated. To deconstruct gender uncritically
and to seek wholly to abolish normative sex categories without attention
to the ways in which black bodies as racially identified have been assaulted
is to risk aligning ourselves with historic white privileging. Being a white
woman or man in America–even only presenting as such–is an inherent
socially powerful and status quo existence.

It is exactly for this reason that it is strange and perhaps even a bit
arrogant for white queers to talk about giving up and doing away with that
from which they have always benefitted, as though such theories ought easily to fit the contexts of persons of color merely because they too happen to
identify as queer. To give up white privilege, which is also gendered stratification–white masculinity being the most privileged–would be solidarity
with the oppressed that is not often demonstrated. On the other hand,
the matter of sex and gender identity is much more complex for African
American queers.

For instance, it is not unusual to hear a Black queer who presents
as biologically female take issue with some stranger who has mistakenly
called them, "Sir." It is not simply a matter of mistaken sexual identity but

11. Moya and Hames-García, eds., *Reclaiming Identity*, 8.

"sir" is interpreted as an insult to one's womanhood[12] and–if that stranger happens to be White–quite possibly interpreted to be another racist attack on the black body. Womanhood expressed in normative femininity is an attribute many (but not all) Black queer women have struggled to possess and maintain within their own families and/or communities. Because gender performance is so critical to the psychological well-being of children growing up within the black community, by the time a Black queer female has reached adulthood she has fought many battles–literally, figuratively, and emotionally–to survive gender oppression and be a healthy and whole individual. Add to this pain sexism and racism, then something as innocent as mistaken identity–the "sir"–is likely perceived as yet another intentional bigoted attack.

Moreover, for Black queers, the term *gay* is too closely identified with white males and white culture. Black queers do not easily embrace the term because it is too aligned with the politics of the '70s gay rights movement that often overlooked the struggles of Black gay men.

As a Black female who has felt the sting of bigotry which devalues the black body, I am convinced that of all the other "isms" with which Blacks must deal, sexual identification utilizing a term that has been relegated–by homophobic heterosexuals–simply to mean romping around in the bedroom is not something done without serious thought. While coming out as "gay" is generally problematic for all queers, coming out and celebrating it in parade-fashion subjects Black queers to a myriad of unique challenges given the cultural pervasiveness of homophobia within the Black community and the extent of racism against people of color even within the queer community.

The long history of African bodies as subjects of attack and denigration by Western and also Eastern culture as well as black bodies being viewed as exotic mystery, cursed mutations, and the lowest of the Western world's bodily caste system are all part of the racist traditions that make "gay pride" a weighty and courageous journey that many Black queers have yet to take. For these reasons and more, though they are small steps, Black queers are rethinking the indiscriminate use of labels and synonyms especially when applied to their lives.

With all these complexities in mind, in this writing I have tried to use the term "queer" not as synonymous with the all-inclusive gay designation

12. Admittedly, this could be perceived as affirmation for the transman (a woman who has changed her physical sexual identity to that of a man).

but as a way of speaking about gay men, lesbian women, bi-sexual, trans-sexual, and intersexed persons in ways that do not limit—as does "gay"–our lives to the intimacy of love-making nor the attractions we may or may not have to persons who share similar genitalia. I use it also specifically to address the queer reality of the lives of Black persons who may self-identify with any of the aforementioned terms, who may or may not identify with heteronormative gender and sex categories but who nonetheless understand themselves as nonheterosexual in their sexual practice and gendered lifestyles. That is to say, I am also speaking about those Black folks who consider themselves to be straight but who participate in same-sex acts.

In addition, though it brings to memory a painful history for some, the term "queer," as it is used now, is a rejection of its tragic and oppressive usage. What we thought we knew about queer, as terminology and anthropology, not only is being turned upside down but also is being shuffled side-to-side, left to right, and cast between dimensions of ontological oughtness. Although we are sexual beings, the queer life has to do with so much more. To the extent that we live, move, and have being, queer life should be understood to encompass the whole of human behavior.

Finally, describing oneself as queer in the African American context in some respects can be thought of as *signifying*. We are taking what was insulting and are embracing it and performatively throwing it back out so as to *read*[13] those who would dare insult us.

In her work, *Signifying, Loud-talking and Marking*, Claudia Mitchell-Kernan defines *signifying* in this way:

> The Black concept of *signifying* incorporates essentially a folk no-tion that dictionary entries for words are not always sufficient for interpreting meanings or messages, or that meaning goes beyond such interpretations. Complimentary remarks may be delivered in a left-handed fashion. A particular utterance may be insult in one context and not another. What pretends to be informative may intend to be persuasive.[14]

For public and academic discourse, as a womanist scholar my convic-tion is also to take on and throw back out the term "queer" as a theological examination. Just as theology is God-talk, womanist queer theology *signifies*

---

13. To "read" someone is an act of verbally "setting someone straight." (No pun in-tended.) It is a response to an insult, a response so cutting and often so embarrassing that the offender will think twice before issuing any other insult. ,

14. Mitchell-Kernan, "Signifying, Loud-talking and Marking," 309–30.

as well as examines basic doctrines and traditions and various queer per-spectives to those doctrines and traditions. I use the term to *signify* because my ultimate goals are to inform and persuade others to do the work of eradicating discrimination of queer persons.

CHAPTER 4

The Biblical Crisis

God For Us

ONTOLOGICAL ARGUMENTS OR DEBATES about the existence of God are ageless. I shall not take up that centuries-old debate in this chapter. However, I do think it is important at least to speak about God if this book is to be considered a text that takes seriously the task of doing theology. Indeed, this is what distinguishes queer theology from queer theory. The primary aim of this chapter is an interrogation of the ways in which *queers of faith* seek understanding about God. Its secondary aim is to address the doctrines of the Christian faith as often framed within orthodox accounts.

Starting with the primary aim: like orthodox traditions, womanist Christian queers understand God as the Divine Creator of all that is, the Cause of All Being. We speak of God primarily by articulating God's activity. We believe, as Karl Barth once said, "When we ask questions about God's being, we cannot in fact leave the sphere of His action and working as it is revealed to us in His Word. God is who He is in His works."[1]

Experience, then, is an essential source for doing queer womanist theology. Even when the Kantian-like cliché is spoken, "God is good all the time and all the time God is good" the chief point (whether we agree or not) is based on our understanding of the work of God in our lives. That is to say, the statement "God is good" is framed as an affirmation of what God has done. In fact, very often the cliché is followed up with *prima facie* testimonies such as, "He woke me up this morning! Ain't God good?" or

---

1. Barth, *Church Dogmatics,* 260.

the longstanding refrain in Black churches, "He put food on my table and clothes on my back. Our God is a good God. Yes, he is!"

The hypothesis is that God the Divine Creator created the world *ex nihilo*. God revealed God's self through the work of Creation. This entity, expressed as Spirit in the Hebrew Bible, formed the world as we know it out of nothing: "the earth was a formless void."[2] This is consistent with our idea of divinity: the capacity to behave and to do what mere mortals cannot. God formed the orderly, determinate world and did so with no preexisting material. God made material earth out of nothing and placed humanity on this land that had at one point been nothingness. This is why we must begin with Creation, because our lives and our understanding of God cannot be separated from that point. It is as creatures and benefactors of the providential, creative work of God that we speak of God. As was articulated in a 1976 article in *The Christian Century*, we understand God to *be* by what God *does* and has done in our created world and by extension in our lives.

> When empiricism is used to seek out and interpret the data about God, we begin with the statement that God *is* what God *does*. Revelation has to do with events and not propositions. Therefore, we identify God with the creative order of the world, a process which transforms human beings, brings values from a potential to an actual state, and works to overcome evil with good. God is that process by which we are made new, strengthened, directed, comforted, forgiven, saved, and by which we are lured into feelings of wonder, awe and reverence.[3]

We believe God reveals God's self to us through events in our lives that are consistent with the ordering of Creation, the work of creating that which God called "good." Womanists have always believed that we come to know God by our experience of God. Therefore, from the writings of our founding womanist scholars, it has always been argued that theology, if it is to be efficacious, must be done from the context of the experience of the oppressed.[4] In that vein, queer womanist theology proposes that any

2. Genesis 1:1 NRSV. I am aware of the creation *out of nothing* vs. creation as the *ordering of chaos* debate. I chose the former interpretation because it is the one most articulated, especially within Black churches.

3. Miller, "Empiricism and Process Theology," 284–87. At the time of this article, Dr. David Miller taught classes at the Stirling Media Research Center, Stirling University, Scotland.

4. See Jacquelyn Grant's chapter, "Women's Experience as The Context and Source for Doing Theology," in Grant, *White Women's Christ and Black Women's Jesus*.

theology that does not respect the context of queer Black women has no purpose and is therefore dead. We have found the academy and Church to be reservoirs of dead theology that refused to drink from the liberating theological perspectives of any source that was not derived by the status quo. And so they died of dehydration, unable to survive in our oasis of critical reflection, and are dead to us not because they failed to become experts of other theological particularities but because they failed at least to dip into our pools of thought. To put it bluntly, using the words of one contemporary African American woman featured on the Internet, "Ain't nobody got time for that!"[5]

In addition to accepting the diverse cultural perspectives about God, if our talk about God has any claims to truth it must be able to connect this talk of our various lived experiences in a way that decisively demonstrates our utter dependence on God and God's utter love for us as mortal imperfect beings. That experience is mysterious at times, and yet we know it as an act of God because it is good beyond human capability.

Unfortunately, all too often prior to developing a healthy conceptualization of God, Black lesbians must contend with experiences and training that tells them not only that God is made in the image of their oppressor but that God hates them categorically. Such was the case of writer, journalist, and daughter of a minister, Ta'Shia Asanti, who recalls her early theological training in this way: "As an adolescent, I was taught the two most important things a budding Black lesbian should know about God: that God is White and Male and that God hates homosexuals. I got it—White men ruled the earth and God would never accept me. That's a hard pill to swallow when you're twelve years old."[6]

Asanti had an interaction with someone who challenged that unhealthy training and provoked her to rethink what she had been taught. That external probing helped her overcome her fear of God.

> Ten years later, the whole experience landed me in therapy and later, twelve-step programs . . . Finally, at a workshop centered around the God thing, a little-bitty, shit-taking sistah named Donna T. asked me the question that changed my life. "How many people here fear God?" she said tipping her head to the side like she always did when she was sharing some deep stuff. "I do," I thought to myself. "All good Christians fear God." "Well you can't

5. Kimberly "Sweet Brown" Wilkins, April 10, 2012

6. Asanti, "Black Lesbians & God: Our Search for Spirituality," 26.

trust and fear anything at the same time. The fear will always cause you to hold some part of yourself back," she said, smiling widely and cocking her head to the side again. I was moved by her revelations . . . Currently, I simply believe that God is love.[7]

It is because we have experienced and know God as love that Black queer womanists must dismiss as heretical any theology that purports that God gives us up to the powers of evil, and leaves us to fend for ourselves. Bishop Yvette Flunder, African American lesbian, said it well, "Church encourages self-loathing."[8] But our experience with God—rather than how homophobic Black preachers have interpreted the text– demonstrates over and over again that God loves us just as we are, in our self-identity and in our living out that identity.

This does not mean that we know all there is to know of God through works, or our experience of God's works alone. We also know God as revealed to us in scripture. Queer Black Christian women believe *there is a word from the LORD*, indeed a *liberating* word from the LORD, and that that word can often be found in the Bible. We turn to the biblical witness with deep respect for its authoritative function in the churches and communities in which we worship and live.

Christian progeny of the African Diaspora living in America have inherited a religious ethos shaped by the ancient Christianity that existed in Africa (especially Egypt) long before the Maafa and in defiance of the exegesis of white Christians who read the text and interpreted the scriptures to them in ways that sought to ensure their captivity. The *invisible institution*,[9] the "folk religion of the slave community," shaped in both the institutional and visible churches and those invisible secret churches of the brush arbors[10] according to historian Albert J. Raboteau, was not the Christianity of their slave masters. The slaves, "creatively fashioned a Christian tradition to fit their own peculiar enslavement in America."[11] Many who were unable to read the Bible memorized cherished verses "by heart." Many heard verses such as Colossians 3:22–24, cherry-picked by slave masters

7. Ibid.

8. "Yvette Flunder, Dispelling the Myth."

9. See Albert J. Raboteau's classic, *Slave Religion: The "Invisible Institution" in the Antebellum South*.

10. Ibid., 210.

11. Ibid., 209.

and used in sermons by Black slaves "authorized" as plantation preachers or white preachers, but refused to receive such texts as authorized by God.

> 22 Servants, obey in all things your masters according to the flesh; not with eyeservice, as menpleasers; but in singleness of heart, fearing God: 23 And whatsoever ye do, do it heartily, as to the LORD, and not unto men; 24 Knowing that of the Lord ye shall receive the reward of the inheritance: for ye serve the LORD Christ.[12]

Instead, it was the textual images of a forsaken, brutally beaten and crucified Jesus Christ that invoked the allegiance of the slaves. Texts that declared the love of God through Jesus, who, like the slaves, was subject to lashes and "lynching," held their attention. Because of his resurrection and power over Creation, texts about the life of Christ, his ministry and miracles for the oppressed, gave Black slaves hope not only for the world to come but also for the world in which they lived. Years after being emancipated, slaves like Howard Thurman's grandmother still refused to hear biblical texts used as propaganda to keep them subservient and in bondage. His illiterate grandmother, to whom Thurman, read the Bible, did not allow him to read her any passages from the Pauline epistles except I Corinthians 13.

> . . . I asked her one day why it was that she would not let me read any of the Pauline letters. What she told me I shall never forget. "During the days of slavery," she said, "the master's minister would occasionally hold services for the slaves. Old man McGhee was so mean that he would not let a Negro minister preach to his slaves. Always the white minister used as his text something from Paul. At least three or four times a year he used as a text: 'Slaves be obedient to them that are your masters . . . as unto Christ.' Then he would go on to show how it was God's will that we were slaves and how, if we were good and happy slaves, God would bless us. I promised my Maker that if I ever learned to read and if freedom ever came, I would not read that part of the Bible."[13]

Some queers wonder why Africans of the Diaspora (which includes Blacks and African Americans) give credence to the Bible at all. The easy response is to say that it feeds our souls. The more reflective response is this: we who were raised as Christians within the Black community often practiced reading skills with the Bible in hand, were made to read scriptures to understand our moral, social, and political responsibilities, were nurtured

12. King James Version as would have been used in antebellum slavery.

13. Thurman, *Strange Freedom*, 144.

under Black preaching styles rich in biblical instruction, and were required to memorize scriptures for our day-to-day living. Queer Black Christians can also interpret the scripture, "Where can I flee from thy spirit . . ." (Psalm 139:7) as "Where can I go where scripture is not present?"

Since most Black Americans belong to some religious tradition or say that religion is important in their lives, and since 78% (at last survey) of the total African American population are Protestant,[14] it is nearly impossible to live in the African American context without persistent reference to God and the Bible, especially if you live in the Bible Belt. Scripture is not only a written instrument but also a way of life for many African Americans, queers included. We turn to the Bible for comfort, guidance, and nurture.

When the late bisexual Caribbean-American writer June Jordan was diagnosed with breast cancer, she turned to the Bible and to a text she remembered from her childhood for comfort and to help her articulate the love she felt from friends who were caring for her around the clock. "And on and on for several months. And I thought, 'This is the love of women. This is the mighty love that is saving my life. And where are the public instances of praise and celebration of this love?' And I found my Bible, and when I could read again, I looked up the story of Ruth to see if I could make sense of it now. And I could. And I did."[15]

For Jordan, this text, which stayed with her from her childhood, contained the "only memorable, and even startling, thoughts attributed to any woman of the Bible."[16] For many young girls and I dare say women, the pericope of Ruth 1: 16–17 was and is one of the most encouraging of all texts. As a queer lesbian woman, the power of this text to speak to the power of what we understand as "woman love" is immense. It encourages us to stand up, to take ownership of our lives even when times are tough. The loyalty of Ruth to her mother-in-law is what we hope to receive and to give to those whom we love dearly. The relationship of Ruth and Naomi symbolizes the kind of steadfast love we hope for our own lives.

Because of these attributes, this text and other biblical texts that convey the beauty of love are often used in commitment ceremonies and same-sex marriages of queer women. I had the pleasure of co-officiating a same-sex marriage between two loving persons, one African American, the other White, at the 4-H Center in Chevy Chase, Maryland on August

14. Pew, "Religious Portrait of African Americans."

15. Jordan, "One Love," in Jordan, *Affirmative Acts*, 76.

16. Ibid., 72.

31, 2013. Mary Ann Kaiser,[17] a candidate for ordination as deacon in The United Methodist Church and Annanda Barclay, Presbyterian and seminary student at Austin Presbyterian Theological Seminary, celebrated their wedding with a liturgy filled with biblical passages. Their understanding of God is rooted in their understanding of scripture and they did not hesitate to turn to the Bible as a viable resource with which to solemnize their marriage.

Scripture has a beautiful way of touching our lives and of helping us survive and thrive in the midst of oppression and the vicissitudes of life. However, the doctrine of *sola scriptura*—the Bible as the unadulterated, inerrant, infallible word of God that contains "those things which are necessary to be known, believed, and observed, for salvation"[18]–must be judged by each Christian generation for its capacity to speak truth to the conditions of its lives. Though doctrines have been derived from the Bible, doctrines are not necessarily the word of God. They are the teaching of the Church that guides adherents in the practices and living out of the faith. The doctrine of *sola scriptura* is a fallible doctrine. And yet this doctrine should not be cast aside wholesale for it has a history that is worth noting for queer Christians, Protestants and Catholics alike.

The value placed on scripture for Black queers (remember they are predominantly Protestant) has a history steeped in the Reformation tradition of the early slave masters. In protest against the abuses (especially the sale of indulgences) within the early Roman Catholic Church, leaders of the Reformation such as Martin Luther, John Calvin, and Huldrych Zwingli, declared that scripture alone, rather than the papacy and the church tradition they espoused, would judge the believer. Most important, that interpretation of the scriptures did not necessitate the help of the Church or Pope. It is this theme of *sola scriptura* that resonates with many African Americans. In fact, we are often reminded to, "let the scriptures speak for themselves."

While some continue this rather elementary approach to interpreting the Bible and allowing it to guide their lives, many Protestants have found their spiritual practices significantly affected by Enlightenment hermeneutical approaches and most specifically historical-critical exegesis.[19] This method, also rooted in the Protestant Reformation, attempts to get

---

17. Mary Ann now identifies as M and prefers pronouns "they/them/their."

18. MacPherson, *Westminster Confession of Faith*, 38.

19. Here we can easily refer back to the empirical methodology of Immanuel Kant.

at the author's original meaning. Applying critical analysis to understand the history and context of the text, the resulting observations are now part and parcel of the theological articulations of both scholars and laypersons, though not always with the same sophistication and certainly not wholly embraced by many in the pews of Black churches.

For instance, African Americans scoff at the idea of a literal interpretation of Colossians 3: 22–24. They suggest one needs to "remember that had to do with how slavery worked during Jesus' days" which is a form of socio-historical criticism. Others may employ *traditional literary criticism*, and seek out the varied meanings of words or an evaluation of the ancient Hebrew or, in this case, Greek form of the text and how the current *translation(s)* have erred. Our more conservative Protestants justify their interpretive take with the notion that "we are operating under a new dispensation," a new era in God's dealings with humanity. In this new dispensation, what took place "in Bible times," while true for then does not entirely hold true for contemporary times. And from here they pick and choose according to their own fundamentalist ideologies.

Their hermeneutics are all well and good until queer Christians posit the same or similar methodologies. When lesbians, gays, bisexuals, and queers refuse to accept a literal interpretation of the few scriptures that have to do with what some consider the "sin of homosexuality," they are criticized for not "accepting the truth of God's word" and for attempting to distort or "exchange the truth with a lie." We are accused of *eisegesis*, of reading our own opinions and experiences *into* the text in contrast to exegesis, which attempts to *pull out* meaning from the text.

In fact, no reader of the text *enters* it *tabula rasa*. We enter the reading of the early Hebrews context and first-century Palestine through the lens of our own twenty-first-century contexts, experiences, and the traditions of our various cultures. To declare a pure, unbiased interpretation belies the arrogant attempt to sit as paragons of Christian virtue. Therefore, to maintain that scripture alone is infallible and the sole source for informing our practice of our faith and our theology is untenable for queer womanist theology. It should come as no surprise that because the text has often been used to oppress queer Black lesbians, we resolutely guard our spiritual lives against the attacks of Bible thumpers.

An example of Black lesbians' regard for the text can be seen in the data collected and published in 2010 by psychotherapist D. Dionne Bates. In her research, Bates interviewed African American lesbians and bisexual women in the southeastern Bible Belt region of the United States who were once married to men. Under the theme "Judge Not, That Ye Not Be Judged," Bates lists several interviews of respondents verbatim who "recalled how the belief system and negative attitudes about sexuality within the church contributed to their internal strife and fear while coming to terms with their lesbian or bisexual identity."[20] Although her work explores identity development and the process of coming out, Dr. Bates did see religion as having significant impact on these women's self-understanding. In her work she regards Black churches as "a corner stone of the African American community."[21]

The reflections of the respondents demonstrate how reason as a resource for theological reflection is a vital element for maintaining wholesome relationship with God, particularly when one's church or family interprets scripture in ways that denigrate one's very being:

> I have a personal relationship with God, so I have to answer for me. . . . I came to the realization that I have my relationship with God . . . and I'm not going to let no one cast stones, because he that cast stones should [. . .] be without any sins. (Respondent 2)

> But, there's always the thing of having grown up in a religious family or in the church, so you deal with what the Bible says . . . of course religion made it difficult. Like I said, when you deal with religion you're dealing with a book and you deal with other people's thoughts, expectations, and rules. You're dealing with the external. (Respondent 5)[22]

The two respondents are able to use reason and scripture to obstruct the "casting of stones" against their character and to understand how societal norms and interpretations of scripture construct and affect one's social location. They apply a real sense of personal agency and a hermeneutics of suspicion to a reading of the text that implies that the only way to know God and be in right relationship with God is to deny one's own rational capacity and instead be subject to the interpretation of scripture given by others "external" to your essential situation.

Having said this, the goal of a queer framing using womanist methodology is not to lift reason above scripture in a way that asserts it as having

20. Bates, "Once-Married African-American Lesbians and Bisexual Women," 211.

21. Ibid.

22. Ibid.

an authoritative function over scripture. Rather, it is to demonstrate how reason appeals to scripture in making theological arguments and to make clear that such arguments about God (and revelation) cannot be grounded in scripture alone.

Indeed, if our only source for knowing God is scripture then God would also be *responsible* for evil because scripture contains accounts of God's behavior that, literally read, are nothing more than barbaric. The same God who is described in the biblical text as "I WILL BE WHAT I WILL BE," indicating God's action, is the same God who as Moses is on his way back to Egypt tries to kill him because he had failed to have his son circumcised![23]

What this means is that we cannot rely solely on what has been written in the Biblical text–what humans had to say about God—in our theological task of speaking about God since to do so would be to stand outside of solidarity with the stories, if also taken literally, of the many persons of color within the text, including Zipporah whom the deity has harmed or instructed be harmed. Elevating the text to be the sole source for knowing God is idolatrous and dangerous for people who say they love God. How can I love God and uncritically love those portions of the text that support genocide of entire people (Joshua 6: 17–21), that condone rape (Deuteronomy 22:28), speak of revenge by dashing one's enemies babies against rocks (Psalm 137:9), and that condone slavery (Col. 3:22)? Had Christian African Americans so exalted the Bible over their belief in the goodness of God, there would have been few if any escapes and no slaves singing, "Befo' I be a slave I be buried in muh grave an' go home ta be wid muh Lord!" We understand that not everything about God has been recorded by humanity and that therefore God stands within and outside the text. We love the Bible for its ability to touch our lives in deep ways, we love its metaphorical and poetic language, we seek daily to live out its deeper meaning for our lives, but we also understand that the Bible is not God.

Womanist biblical scholar and queer ally, Dr. Mitzi J. Smith offered these very helpful words about God and the Bible in a recent Facebook conversation:

---

23. Exodus 4:24–26: "On the way, at a place where they spent the night, the LORD met him and tried to kill him. But Zipporah took a flint and cut off her son's foreskin, and touched Moses' feet with it, and said, 'Truly you are a bridegroom of blood to me!' So he let him alone. It was then she said, 'A bridegroom of blood by circumcision.'"

God . . . was before, after and transcends the Bible. The Bible is written not even in the first human language. How do you give the same authority to God that you give to the Bible. [sic] If you do so you have to subordinate all human experience with the divine outside of the text to the Bible too. The Bible is certainly not my authority when it comes to my calling as a female preacher or as a black person with slave ancestors. Also you have to discount the fact that the Bible must be translated;[sic] that before it was translated into the languages of the common people, access was limited and where was God the authority of God.[sic] It the [sic] hands, according to the church of the few who had access and were determined by themselves to be the authoritative interpreters. No my friend God lives. The text is only living as God gives it life. . . . But God's Word is not limited to the Bible, is the point . . . God spoke before the Bible, and God speaks today. The Bible is a witness to the fact that God spoke and speaks. It [sic] does contain all that is God or God's Word! Is [sic] your God that small and that limited in speech! [sic]. . . you search the scriptures because IN THEM, you think you find eternal life, BUT they testify about me." John 5:39.. in other words eternal life is in God/Jesus and NOT the Text[24]

As queers, we declare that God cannot be limited. God is not finite. God is not determinate as are we created beings. Therefore, as Smith argues, God cannot be made subordinate to human experience or to the text written and interpreted by humans. As Bishop Carlton Pearson likes to say, "The Bible is the inspired word of men about God."

Thankfully, because of human reason—another source for queer womanist theological work—we need not rely on the Bible alone. In fact, we understand the God of the Bible *because* of human reason, by our ability to think and do critical reflection. This ability to know God via reason is so important it is listed in the catechism of the Catholic Church and the various writings of the early Church Fathers. They understood that scripture simply cannot be properly interpreted without reason. So important was reason as a source for doing theology among Methodists that it is listed among what is often referred to as the Wesleyan quadrilateral: reason, experience, scripture, and tradition.

For instance, using reason one could interpret from Paul's letter to Christian believers in Rome that same-sex loving attraction is God's

24. Dr. Mitzi J. Smith, Facebook, October 7, 2013

punishment upon persons who worshiped idols.[25] Moreover one could say that this passage is really a divine charge against heterosexual persons doing what is not natural *for them* sexually. The interpretation could be: "Because heterosexuals chose to use their bodies in service to the idolatrous culture of their times, God gave them up to engage in passions, in intercourse that was unnatural for them." The strongest assessment that can be made of this pericope is that it is the writer's opinion about how God has meted out punishment against the wicked, that is, that the wicked behave in this way because God has given them up to their debased minds. If we must continue this logic, then what of this challenge—a question I really take exception to but has nonetheless been asked: If homosexuality is the resulting "punishment" of God giving up on individuals who have determined not to "retain God in their mind," then should not all devout atheists be homosexuals? I imagine the literalist would respond negatively and justify his or her response, perhaps in the way that my Pentecostal colleagues suggest: "Not every person who says they are atheists are *really* atheists. They still have some measure of the truth in them and God is still working with them."

I offer this example to suggest that even applying reason to scripture is not sufficient to the task of theology and, to use an old addage, "Honest people will disagree." If we are gracious with one another, we will admit our inadequacies as interpreters of the text and concede that some things will remain mystery throughout our lives *on this side of Jordan*, as we often say in Black churches. The meaning: In this life, we know only in part. It is only at the end of time, the eschaton, when our knowledge shall be whole.

Like all hermeneutic work, our interpretation is never perfect but a work in progress. We must constantly strive to understand not only what appears to be a "given" meaning but the deeper meanings within the text. We need to ask probing questions of the text and context. We must always take into account, as best we can ascertain, the diverse vantage points represented by those who recorded their accounts of the events that took place during and before their time. There is simply no one simple and exact reading of the text and its events, which is why, for example, you have several versions of singular events such as Jesus' birth and Creation.

---

25. "Therefore God gave them up in the lusts of their hearts to impurity, to the degrading of their bodies among themselves, because they exchanged the truth about God for a lie and worshiped and served the creature rather than the Creator, who is blessed forever! Amen." Romans 1:24–25.

My conservative colleagues will say that this results in relativism and ultimately apostasy or heresy. If, in fact, queer womanists argued that all of life including all that we consider to be real is subjective and arbitrary, then we would certainly be guilty of relativism. If we posited all of scripture to be subjective, again, we would be guilty of relativism. However, our critique is not about the ultimate truth of scripture but about how one comes to declare what is true and what should be regarded as true. As womanists we refuse to allow any and everybody to define what is truth and especially if they do so solely to maintain some sense of "orthodoxy." Our history as progeny of slaves living in a world that continues to discriminate against black bodies and bodies of color, has taught us the fallacy of believing our oppressor's truth.

As Christians working towards the realization of the Beloved Kindom, we strive daily towards the Ultimate Truth, courageously *yielding* to the presence of ambiguities in this life. In this regard, queer womanists are more pragmatists than relativists or objectivists. Admittedly, like many liberals and human rights advocates I lean towards meliorism.[26]

Queer Black Christians hold on to the text trusting that it will inspire us—through the truth, which we are able to glean from it for our lives—to be better people working to make the world a more just and peaceable place.

It is also important to rely upon reason to ponder the ways and being of God. Critical reflection can be very rewarding and is beautifully demonstrated when queer Black women, rather than allow segments of the institutional church to harm them psychologically and spiritually with unhealthy theology, dig deep into their spiritual sense to maintain the idea of a relational God who transcends the kind of religious bias they hear.

Queer womanists Christians can also employ Holy Tradition (not traditionalism) as a source for our theological task. Holy Tradition is those teachings of the Church that have been handed down. Our confessions, doctrine, creeds, and liturgy are good examples of Holy Tradition. For instance, we take seriously the Apostles' Creed and seek to understand how its pronouncements have affected the lives of Black LBTQ members of the Christian faith. The rich history of the miracles wrought through prayer and the stories of how our ancestors relied on prayer is inspirational and spiritually vital. We understand also how confession can be both healing

26. See the work of pragmatist William James.

for the soul and how it can be destructive to the spirit when yielded as an instrument of ungracious rebuke.

Through the benefit of the gift of Holy Tradition we are also aware of how other teachings handed down to persons of other faith traditions affect not only their lives but ours as well. As African Americans, we are especially hoping to learn more of the traditions, theology, and sacred texts of our queer womanist colleagues not of the Christian faith. We respect voodun, Yorùbá, Santería, Candomblé, Islam, Judaism, Buddhism, and African Traditional Religion though we have only a small but growing understanding of them made possible by our relationship in the womanist circle of "the folk."

Finally, all four sources–scripture, reason, experience and tradition– are important for queer womanist theology because they help substantiate our faith. They are not, however, the foundation of our faith. The foundation of our faith is God and it is in our trust in God that we find sufficient response to the mysteries of life.

Currently, one of those mysteries of life is in the very being of lesbian, bisexual, transgender, and queer persons. Our sexuality is a mystery to which scientists and other life "experts" have no factual response. They do not "know" why or how we are as we self-identify. Nature or nurture? Lifestyle or life? There has not yet been found evidence to categorically attribute how we come to be or understand our sexual identity and expression. Mystery.

Most Christian arguments that attempt to respond to the elements of our lives use some combination of scripture, reason, experience, and tradition to substantiate their claims. Together, they are powerful resources for articulating what we believe is God's will for our lives. God, as *mysterium tremendum et fascinans*[27] and *soul-lover* is the foundation of our faith. God is mystery that provokes both fear and fascination in us. God is also the lover of our souls who touches us deep down within our very being. Even with the best of our resources, there are elements of God's created world that are beyond our ken.

The current crisis of the Church surrounding sexuality will continue because our conversations are often not guided by faith but by the will to control. This will, at its core, springs forth from fear of the unknown. Unfortunately, when discussing sexuality too many Christians of all stripes fail to put to full use all theological sources and fail to enter the discussion

27. Term accredited to German theologian Rudolph Otto from his book, *Das Heilige*.

humbly. Mostly, what they do is apply scripture not in order to *find out* but in order to *tell why*. This is oppression clothed in religiosity. Guided by fear of sexuality, the ultimate human existential unknown condition, we dig deep into our positions and refuse simply to say, "I don't know." Admitting what we don't know will free us to work with what we do know. Because we don't fully understand human sexuality, what can we do with what we know? Begin by loving ourselves as God has created us.

CHAPTER 5

Co-Caretakers of
a Bountiful Blessing

As I write, protestors have taken to the streets in Ferguson, Missouri, outraged by the shooting of unarmed African American teenager Michael Brown by a white policeman. I have made several visits to Ferguson in the midst of the protest. I felt I needed to be there, as a Black woman, as ordained clergy, and as a scholar. I wanted to lend my support to the protestors and I wanted to do so with a womanist appreciation for the struggle, in the strong belief that without this struggle justice would not prevail. This chapter, both a sociological and theological reflection, centers on my experiences in Ferguson and the primary question that derived from that experience: How does one overcome the impact of years or decades of oppression without being overtaken by a bitterness of the soul? Critically reflecting upon this question is not only important for Black people but–with regard to this manuscript–also Black LGBTQ persons who suffer under multiple levels of oppression.

I will also explore this question in light of my understanding of the doctrine of creation. I do believe that how we see ourselves in relation to God's good Creation has something to do with how we see ourselves in relation to each other. Black people's response or lack of response to oppression is part of the ongoing historical saga of our country. I had the pleasure of doing research in the archives of the late episcopal priest, Pauli Murray. My interest was sparked by several readings about the remarkable extent she went to, including surgery, to prove her attraction to women was not due to lesbianism but because she was actually a man trapped in a woman's body.[1] Her own journal entries reveal that she considered herself to be a biological man and as one with an "inverted sex instinct."[2] When I think of Pauli Murray's tragic story of sexual identity I honor her journey knowing countless queer and transgender persons who benefit from her work to end sexism and discrimination, though she herself did not live to enjoy such freedom of expression.

Despite and perhaps because of being the object of discrimination, Murray became an activist for racial and gender equality. As an attorney, her work helped shape laws for full inclusion of women and African Americans. Yet Murray would find herself at odds with both white feminists and African Americans. It is her relationship with the latter that I briefly explore in this chapter as Murray was concerned about the hostility she saw Black militant students express. The rage she saw and found so unhealthy in these students is a rage with which I am intimately familiar having grown up in the '60s and '70s. It is a rage I understand, being both Black and a queer lesbian.

In this chapter though I explore the rage of the oppressed, I am more concerned about the bitterness of the soul of the oppressor, how that came to be, and how the oppressed may avoid the same bitterness. I offer no theory to eradicate oppression but I do analyze it from a theological perspective, and frame my analysis within Christian theological anthropology. Ever influenced by my experiences within the Pentecostal Church, I deal largely with the human soul and its relationship to its created self, others, and to its Creator. Most relevant to this work, I am interested in addressing how Black LGBTQ persons can thrive while living with the constant threat of aggression and the constant ethos of oppression within our own Black communities, our own LGBTQ community, and in the larger American society. My womanist curiosity leads me to ponder how womanist thought about the "survival and wholeness of community" can be a supportive referent in the struggle to thrive without being caught in a web of bitterness. To this cause I offer the following reflection and analysis about systemic racism that impacts Black LGBTQ persons now even as it did during Murray's life.

1. See Sarah Azaansky's *The Dream is Freedom: Pauli Murray and American Democratic Faith* and Anne Firor Scott's, *Pauli Murray and Caroline Ware: Forty Years of Letters in Black and White*

2. Murray, Papers, Diary entry, 12/16/1937. Box 4; Folder 71.

On August 19, 2014, I arrived in Ferguson. Some time between my first departure for Ferguson and my arrival, I decided to livestream broadcast my time in Ferguson.[3] I not only wanted to see with my own eyes what was going on, I wanted to offer to others a unique perspective of what was going on, one that would not necessarily be covered by mainstream media. What does it mean to be a theologian whose place for doing theology is within, in alignment and/or perhaps even as participant within the activist movement? Indeed ought the intellectual locate themselves in the struggle through their physical, immediate, on the ground activism? This is the tenor of the questions I asked myself as I sat on the plane headed to Ferguson. Having determined that my livestream activities could not do more than address that specific situation, having been trained in theological ethics, I had plenty of questions about how the immediacy of activist work shapes and drives the theological task.

My work was supported by generous financial support from both Boston University School of Theology and Reconciling Ministries Network, who also sent two of its communications staff. The latter's support was essential because they came with press passes that enabled me to spend time in Ferguson not only recording events but also operating, as far as the local police might be concerned, as a journalist.

The several interviews I livestreamed show the deep pain and anger of the Black community. They and their allies from around the world felt they were witnessing a strategy of intimidation and rogue engagement on the part of many local police officers. Tensions were on the rise. State and federal politicians were brokering conversations between protestors and local city politicians. The frequency with which white police attack and even kill often unarmed black persons has ignited a national outcry among members of the Black community and their allies around the world. People of goodwill understood the danger of allowing this atrocity to continue with impunity. They rightly understood that this brutality could not and cannot be tolerated.

The attacks against Black men and women are symptomatic of systemic racism and also reveal many other areas of discrimination. The nation is now learning of numerous troubling patterns in Ferguson, such as the city profiting from unusually high traffic fines and warrant revenues. How does one pay hundreds of dollars in traffic fines when one's annual

---

3. Pamela R. Lightsey, "Ferguson: BU Womanist Scholar in Action" and "Ferguson: The Decision." August and November 2014.

salary is well below the poverty line? How does one get the money to bail oneself out of jail or to pay for an attorney who will be thoroughly invested in one's defense? While not all persons stopped or arrested by police are innocent, the statistics cannot be ignored and lead any reasonably person to question whether racial discrimination was not being practiced by that local police department. Indeed this is the question that US Attorney General Eric Holder and his team of inspectors are now investigating.

If the federal civil rights probe reveals evidence similar to a report released by former Washington University interns, the nation will know that the mistrust citizens of Ferguson have of the local police department is warranted.[4] They will also marvel at the patience of those citizens for not exploding with anger long before the particular killing of Michael Brown. According to the report, "Municipal Courts White Paper" written by Arch-City Defenders,[5] a legal group reviewing municipal courts in St. Louis county, "Even given Ferguson's large black population, the disparity index shows that black motorists are over-represented in traffic stops."[6] Years of being racially profiled, of being given traffic fine after traffic fine, has compounded their already impoverished conditions, but this is but a fraction of the civil rights violations the Black citizens of Ferguson have endured. For the financial tolls combine with racism and with mass incarceration, and so on and so forth. Oppression on one level intersects with oppressions on other levels. There is no safe quadrant of society if we allow unchecked and unprovoked hostilities to occur against any single community of people. The protests in Ferguson were inevitable. The rage was long in the making.

---

4. After the time of this writing, that report was released. The report detailed what were described as "unconstitutional stops and arrests" and police practices that "undermine community trust." See http://www.justice.gov/sites/default/files/opa/press-releases/attachments/2015/03/04/ferguson_police_department_report.pdf

5. ArchCity Defenders, "Municipal Courts Whitepaper" stated the reason for their research: "ArchCity Defenders has been working in the municipal courts in St. Louis County since 2009. During that time, our clients have described being stopped, harassed, jailed for not being able to pay fines, and feeling as if they were second-class citizens. As a result of this feedback, ACD conducted a court watching program during which we observed 60 courts. While many, many municipal court treated clients well, worked with them on payments, and did not incarcerate them for non-payment of fines, 30–40 of these courts consistently reflected the practices our clients described. We narrowed our study to the municipalities of Bel-Ridge, Ferguson, and Florissant because we heard from our clients and personally observed systemic problems that hurt our clients, the municipality itself, and our region."

6. Ibid.

The details leading up to the protest have been sketchy, but what protestors and the nation does know is horrible: A young 18-year old Black man, Michael Brown, was shot multiple times by a police officer. The killing of this unarmed teenager took place within a few weeks of the killing of an unarmed Black man in New York. Staten Island police strangled to death Eric Garner by an illegal chokehold.[7] Just days after Michael's killing, police in Los Angeles fatally shot Ezell Ford, a 25-year old man who suffered from mental illness, as he lay on his back in full compliance with police orders.[8]

Pictures from the Ferguson protest have a surreal similarity to the protests of the '60s; men carrying "I AM A MAN" signs; police standing against protestors with German Shepherd police dogs; journalists being falsely arrested; and mothers weeping over the death of a child. The images counter the stereotype of "victim mentality" launched against Black people who in fact have the courage to declare that we do not live in a "post-racist" nation, that daily there are countless injustices against Black people. Yet no matter how many images of such racist action are caught on camera, no matter how many sounds of brutality are recorded against black men and women, some people's unreflective default response is to advocate that Black people pull themselves up by their own bootstraps, and they complain of being "tired of Black people whining."

Some such respondents have even gone so far as to make the "nice '60s Negro" comparison, insisting that the '60s era civil rights protestors was nonviolent. They have either forgotten or are ignorant of what took place during the summer of 1965, the six days of Black rage and revolt against Los Angeles Police Department (LAPD) racism called the Watts Riot,[9] and few speak of the history of white mobs looting cities and even the looting of the White House after the assassination of President Lincoln. They compare the looting of Ferguson with their own "good Negro" imagery of the

7. Goodman, "Difficult Decisions Ahead in Responding to Police Chokehold Homicide."

8 Johnson, "Ezell Ford."

9. Like Ferguson, Watts had a largely African American population plagued by unemployment and high rates of incarceration. Similar to Ferguson, the riot in Watts was touched off by a confrontation between a white police officer and a young Black man, Marquette Frye. Both events occurred within the context of an already strained relationship between Black citizens and law enforcement (including the judicial system). Frye was roughed up when stopped for intoxication. He, his brother, and mother were arrested. Their mistreatment at the hands of the police set off six days of rioting during which time people were killed, property was destroyed and looted, a curfew was established, and the National Guard were called in to quell the violence.

nonviolent civil rights protestors. They plug their ears to the reality of the white police officer calling the protestors, "fucking animals."[10]

What motivates Black rage now made visible through our protests, writing, preaching—and yes, looting—are the sustained efforts to control Black people, our lives, our bodies, and our thoughts. White racists don't care about these efforts to care about these efforts to control our own lives and there are some Blacks response of rage as shameful or deviant. What they think should not dictate the outcry; there is a collective state of mind among people who have endured socioeconomic oppression and racial discrimination supported by public policies and authorities that are willfully culpable or unsympathetically complicit. This is the state of mind that remembers riots like Watts and police officers like LAPD Chief William Parker who said, "One person threw a rock and then, like monkeys in a zoo, others started throwing rocks."[11] Almost twenty years after Watts, white police officers are still referring to the citizens they are employed to protect and serve as animals.

The rage of the oppressed that carry the burden of being treated as animals should be understandable when you read reports like The Whitepaper. On a national level, the ongoing reports of violence against Black people by police as well as the available statistics related to mass incarceration of Black men and women has only supported the generalized distrust of law enforcement and the subsequent acts of rage that ensued on a national level. The poet James Baldwin once wrote of our rage saying, "To be Black and conscious in America is to be in a constant state of rage."[12]

Baldwin understood that Black rage is not an irrational outburst but a passionate response to the evil of racism imposed upon us across our lifetimes. It is to be constantly aware, always conscious, of the mistreatment of Black people. Our rage is not because we *seek* examples of injustice but because we have only to open our eyes each morning and turn our gaze toward our segregated communities to see its impact. Whether we live in these communities or have managed to "ascend" the socioeconomic ladder a few rungs and are glancing over into these communities from our suburban negridity, to be consciously Black in America is to have this awareness.

10. The video of this scene was captured by CNN and is found at http://www.huffingtonpost.com/2014/08/12/michael-brown-protests_n_5672163.html.

11. Parker, Interview with *New York Times*.

12. Baldwin, "Negro Leaders on Violence."

Racism in America has been in effect so long that it seems an incorrigible entity. We speak of it as not only as a characteristic but also as a having a life of its own. In some ways it reminds me of the demons the Pentecostal church warned would enter "un-prayed-up" bodies. Yet unlike the demons in the Bible, there appears to be no exorcism to remove it from the soul of our country and even the world.

On a personal level, I have been living with and have been a target of racism since birth. I attended segregated elementary schools and especially remember the fear of being bused outside my neighborhood during the first years of desegregation. These days I reflect upon the fear of racist behavior and the impact it has on the lives of the oppressed. Though many years removed from the upheaval that desegregation brought to my community, I will never forget the palpable sense of fear and helplessness. That fear mixed with an increased sense of the internal rage I had trained myself to reduce to burning embers resurfaced during my two visits to Ferguson during the hot summer days of 2014.

Remembering the racial climate of my youth while marching in protest under the watchful eye of a police and National Guard force that had already used tear gas and wooden bullets on local Ferguson residents gave me good reason to be afraid.[13] That fear, accented by an awareness of the need to direct my rage into some activity or activities with which to support the goals of the protest aligned me with the young adult leaders of the protest. Their defiance, their calculated strategies to maintain national attention on the toxic living conditions white oppression had enforced upon Black Fergusonians was admirable and apparent immediately upon my setting feet on W. Florissant Avenue.

Also apparent was the difference of opinion between older (predominantly male clergy) and young adult activists on the best strategies and tools for the protest. Both groups were calling for the arrest of Officer Wilson, but the young adult activists felt the clergy were being used as an arm of the state. Meetings between area clergy and Ferguson officials to discuss strategies for healing and moving the city forward seemed premature to these young activists and many supporters across the nation. They perceived the

---

13. An excerpt from one article about Palm Beach County desegregation reads: "During the first year of desegregation, 3,300 white students left public school. Some reactions were less passive: a stick of dynamite on a school bus and police in riot gear in Riviera Beach, fires at Twin Lakes High in West Palm Beach, students cut with razors at Boca Raton High, and fistfights and bomb threats at Atlantic High School in Delray Beach." Palm Beach County History Online, "School Desegregation."

nightly prayers of Black clergy followed by instructions for the protestors to disburse as an affront and as a misguided attempt to fix what could not be fixed during the years of slavery, Jim Crow, and current killings. For them, that kind of faith action could not do the work needed to end discrimination based on race. It could not bring justice in Ferguson, especially since it was the militarized police forces that were requesting the nightly prayers.

While the world looked on, young protestors were often depicted as operating under a kind of anomie and volatile Black Nationalism. Admittedly, I attributed my affinity for the young adult protestors to my own history of embracing the Black Power advocates in the '60s and '70s. I understood them not as incorrigible but as justifiably suspicious of strategies that included cooperating with the status quo.

On the other hand, clergy such as Clergy United and those working with PICO, a national faith-based agency, sought to ensure the safety of the protestors, helped to shape the community's written demands for justice, marched in solidarity to the county prosecutor's office, and were on site listening to persons recount their experiences of being traumatized by local law enforcement personnel. There were also clergy who made "peace and calm" the evening goals. Seeing to it that "no trouble breaks out tonight" "let's show them we can do this" were among the urgings spoken by clergy who marched along the inner perimeter of the march. These concerns were largely ridiculed among young activists who accused some of the clergy as being tokens of the state sanctioned aggression against their right to peacefully assemble and protest.

With these differing approaches to gaining justice, I found myself reminiscing on the journal entries of the late Pauli Murray, whom I introduced at the beginning of the chapter. One of the early progenitors of the nonviolent strategy of the civil rights movement, Murray, a civil rights activist, attorney, and professor was in angst over the militancy and abandonment of nonviolent protocol demonstrated by Black students only months after the assassination of Rev. Dr. Martin Luther King, Jr.

> I weep for them, for they are—some of them—like the young Communists of the 1930s clinging to a "God that failed." Their "Black Consciousness" has become a religion to be defended at all costs and in some of the more extreme cases it has a suicidal thrust—they see themselves as the ultimate victims of genocide! . . . How can one make these youngsters see that they are not dealing with a monolithic white society arrayed against them like a consuming fire but that they are dealing with social forces and

structures, some of them impersonal, and that unless they analyze and understand these forces and learn to manipulate or help to control them, they will help to sweep themselves and the rest of us into chaos.[14]

Murray's experiences at Brandeis University, where she served as visiting professor of American Civilization, are recorded in her journals kept at the Schlesinger Library at Harvard University. During her tenure in the late '60s and early '70s, her relationship with African American students was ambivalent. "I am troubled about my relations—not with the Negro students on campus—but with the Black students, a term I am using in a political sense."[15] Murray saw the "Black" students as angry, hostile and having a "suicidal thrust."[16]

In contrast to Murray, I do not consider Black people to be angry enough! Yes, we have risen up in pockets, but large-scale expressions of anger over years of oppression have not happened since the '60s. I am not urging a resurgence of national riots but I do feel resistance growing and necessarily because of the steady diminution of all our work to eradicate racial discrimination. I am surprised neither by the outcry in Ferguson nor by the national outcry that is pregnant in the souls of Black folks. What concerns me is not our anger or hostility but tacit acceptance of our supposed lot in life. This acceptance brews a bitterness and nihilism that threatens the very souls of oppressed people.

How does one respond to years or decades of oppression without being overtaken by a bitterness of the soul?

The starting point for queer womanist reflection upon this question must begin with Creation itself. A hubristic understanding of the world as the work of human hands rather than of God's good Creation is the origination of the first level of oppression, the foundation to all the interlocking oppressions. On this path, humanity substitutes a theological perspective of themselves as caretakers of the world with the belief that they are the owners and sustainers of the world. *Creatio ex nihilo*, the teaching that The Divine formed Earth and Universe from nonexistence, out of nothing, becomes a blurred concept, even an idea not worth pondering. When we believe human beings are the architects rather than the caretakers of Creation the negative cycle of one group elevating themselves above another

---

14. Murray, Papers, Diary entry, 11/1/68.

15. Ibid.

16. Ibid.

based on biological sex difference or particular phenotypes begins and is maintained.

Though I do not take the doctrine of Creation to be anything other than doctrine, and therefore refutable (something I discuss briefly in the next chapter), it is quite helpful to theological reflection. Its premise that the world in which we live originated outside the capability of mortals is one of the sacred tenets of the Christian Church. God as the *first cause* has been a source of hope for Black queer Christians. To understand that this world ultimately does not belong to humanity but to somebody bigger than us has long been a source of hope for Black queer Christians. No matter how oppressive the sermons on Sunday morning, we take courage in the knowledge that our care, our wellbeing, is not dependent on human hands but on the providential care of God our Creator.

It is, after all, the doctrine of Creation that emphasizes that God is not only the Creator of all life and nature but also that God who is distinct, who is transcendent from creation, is also active in the world that has been created. God who ordered the world into being and set precedence by the creation of humanity from dust is relational, then and now. God shaped and breathed life into humanity and did not desire to leave us alone. Having prohibited Adam and Eve from eating from of the one tree of the knowledge of good and evil, God entrusted them with all that was created and charged them to care for every living creature.

Yet even once creation is in the hands of humanity, God does not separate God's self from the world and people God had created. The relational nature of God to the human beings God has created is depicted as being loving and caring. The text paints the image of this loving God walking with humanity and of being in conversation with them. Adam and Eve are conscious of God's presence. They lack no good thing and they have freedom to make decisions for their lives.

This very freedom is defiled in a hubristic moment of disobedience to God's instructions. Turning away from God to eat of the tree of the knowledge of good and evil was an existentially defining point of humanity's own self-injury of the conscious and alienation of the soul. When God walked in the Garden of Eden and called out to Adam asking, "Where are you?,"[17] it was only because God felt humanity turning from that divine relationship to a hubristic, self-centered relationship. This was and is the beginning of oppression.

17. Genesis 3:9 NRSV.

The desire, this hubris, to obtain what God had prohibited at the expense and exclusion of all other gifts can only be actualized when we exchange the truth for a lie. The desire therefore leads to a false understanding of ourselves and of our world, a false consciousness; it is a turning away as theologian Paul Tillich argues:

> Hubris is not one form of sin besides others. It is sin in its total form, namely, the other side of unbelief or man's turning away from the divine center to which he belongs. It is turning toward one's self as the center of one's self and one's world. This turning away toward one's self is not an act done by a special part of man, such as his spirit. Man's whole life, including his sensual life, is spiritual. And it is in the totality of his personal being that man makes himself the center of his world.[18]

Though aware of God's presence, when hubris is at work humanity is conscious of that presence not as the center of our lives but as an appendage of our lives. Once the human situation and relationship with God has shifted in this way, self-elevation and indeed marginalization of others inevitably results.

The oppression of Black people by whites who benefit from self-elevation and marginalization is an old and tragic story. The egregious injustices borne by Black people are real. Period. Not only have we been denied equal access to the benefits white Americans enjoy but white racists are also attempting to change the narrative to make the world and even the oppressed feel as though they are responsible for their own victimization. What is most reprehensible is the sinister berating of Black people who, having every right to be angry, respond with acts of civil disobedience, protest and yes, even riots.

Stripped of our dignity through a calculated police strategy of racial profiling and numerous acts of police brutality, public policies derived to cheat Black people of their hard-earned income, to deny them proper health care and quality education only incites and escalates situations similar to Ferguson across America and throughout our country's history. The anger against oppression is something we absolutely have to express. It is a wonder it takes so long to reach a boiling point. When this unexpressed anger finally reaches its limit, it manifests in an explosive anger that to some seems illogical and unreflective. But Black people have had ample time to "reflect" on their suffering. What is not needed are attempts to calm and

---

18. Tillich, *Systematic Theology*, 2:50–51.

quiet a people who have berated, maligned, and who have watched their loved ones killed because they refused to be regarded as anything less than fully human and fully equal. It is not their anger that ought to shock us but the fallout of human pride that will not see itself as co-caretakers of God's creation. Not the rage of the protestors but the attempted subjugation of other caretakers of God's creation. Unchecked this will always result in destruction—of the earth, of property, and of lives. It is with the unchecked domination and not the unexpressed anger that we must concern ourselves.

Like Murray, I worry about the "consciousness" but not the anger of the oppressed that continually cry out against the odious sin of discrimination. Unexpressed anger leads to a bitterness of the soul and a constant inability to have a de-niggerized self-consciousness. It is imperative that our consciousness, how we understand ourselves as a community, not function as some intractable religious foundation whereby we are doomed always to act as prostrating subjects of oppression suffering from insurmountable persecution. Likewise, the collective consciousness[19] of the oppressed must not interpret contestation against us as justification for militant *non-negotiable* response. The capacity to see the "social forces and structures," as Murray put it, that are at work can only be gained by critical analysis and divorcing ourselves from the temptation to allow our emotions rather than our hearts and minds together to lead the way. How do we avoid a bitterness of the soul through unexpressed or misguided rage? Murray's answer to the problem lies in the spirituality of the people. Of racial violence she said, "I am convinced that the historical strength of the Negro race has come from its ability to transcend that experience and develop a spirituality that was both enduring and resilient."[20]

Within womanist writings there have been many references to Black women's ability to survive the horrors of slavery. Most speak not only of the inner strength of Black women but of her sustaining spirituality. The religion of Black people remains an important resource. The Pew research paper of 2009 entitled, "A Religious Portrait of African Americans," reports on African American women's religiosity (which I translate as spirituality): "African-American women also stand out for their high level of religious commitment. More than eight-in-ten black women (84%) say religion

19. Here I am suggesting the possibility of a common or general consciousness present in many oppressed persons created as a means of survival and taking shape in cultural traditions and ideals.

20. Murray, Papers, Diary entry, 11/1/68.

is very important to them, and roughly six-in-ten (59%) say they attend religious services at least once a week. No group of men or women from any other racial or ethnic background exhibits comparably high levels of religious observance."[21] Religion plays a major role in the lives of Black people with Black women among the most religious people in the country. Some, looking at the problems of substance abuse and high drop out rates, have even suggested that Black people are too observant, too attendant to the church when they should be tending to their immediate communities.

However, church membership is not an essential trait of Black spirituality. Womanists have, for quite some time, accepted and welcomed discussions on Black spirituality over and against organized religion. We understand that spirituality is not contained by doctrines, dogma, denominations, or faith traditions. Indeed, findings from the same Pew report demonstrate just that: "even African-Americans who are unaffiliated with any religion consistently express higher levels of religious beliefs compared with the unaffiliated public overall. Unaffiliated African-Americans, for instance, express certain belief in God (70%) at levels similar to those seen among the general population of mainline Protestants (73%) and Catholics (72%) and are about twice as likely as the overall unaffiliated population (36%) to express this belief.[22]" So, while I situate my comments according to my context as a Christian scholar, I am fully aware that Black spirituality should not be articulated solely on the basis of any one denomination. Black spirituality is deeper than–and can also be absent from—any relationship with the Church universal. Black spirituality, especially Black women's spirituality, is connected to our very being. We may even speak of it as "my spirituality." Where I am, there also is my spirituality, my sense of my connectedness to Spirit.

Emilie Townes has given an excellent description of womanist spirituality: "Womanist spirituality is not grounded in the notion that spirituality is a force, a practice separate from who we are moment by moment. It is the deep kneading of humanity into one breath, one hope, one vision. Womanist spirituality is not only a way of living, it is a style of witness that seeks to cross the yawning chasm of hatreds and prejudices and oppressions into a deeper and richer love of God as we experience Jesus in our lives."[23] Womanist spirituality as "our way of living" and a "style of witness" is precisely

21. Pew Forum, "Religious Portrait of African Americans."
22. Ibid.
23. Townes, *In a Blaze of Glory*, 11.

those ingredients that have helped many Black women transcend the works of oppression, particularly dehumanization and discrimination.

An abiding spirituality that helps a people avoid a bitterness of the soul takes shape and thrives in relationship with God. It is nurtured not by self-abnegation but by a humbleness of heart that does not deny the world is under the authority of God rather than the lordship of humanity. It does not require a formal liturgy, dogma, or denomination. This spirituality is both organic and learned. It has been passed on by sitting at the feet of the elders, by listening to them recount "how we got over," by observing them survive each crisis of life.

And yet, racism thrives on a bitterness of the soul that has been alive since antiquity. It is the same bitterness that smothered Cain's soul. Having succumbed to the pride that demands self-aggrandizement and elevation above mutual relationship, it was Cain who lured his brother to the field and committed the first act of physical murder. His parents had already committed a kind of "killing" of the spirit by their own willingness to disobey God's life-giving instructions. Like his parents who allowed a shift in their relationship with God, Cain yielded to the temptation of pride, which in turn led to jealousy of his brother. Once jealousy had established its roots in his soul it could yield nothing short of bitter fruit. This bitterness is alienation disguised as self-determination. It is the alienation of the soul that does not cherish relationship with God or with Creation. White racism is the bitterness of the soul that declares whiteness to be superior, that prejudges a people, and concomitantly supports (consciously or subconsciously) those systems and structures that deny them basic human rights equal to your own.

Similarly, homophobia is a bitterness of the soul that demonizes and seeks to subjugate, and in extreme cases, even murder LGBTQ persons. Like racism, homophobia is not solely an attitude but it can lead to frightening behavior. Data available from the FBI national hate crime statistics report of 2012 reveals the horrible consequences of homophobia acted out against LGBTQ persons. The rate of attacks against LGBTQ persons is second only to racially motivated attacks. Of the 7,164 reported victims of hate crimes, 48.5 % were targeted due to race while 19.2% were targeted due to perceived sexual orientation.[24] Matters are much worse for female LBTQ persons. If you review the 2012 FBI national incident report under the table entitled "Crimes Against Persons," you immediately see the overwhelming

24. FBI, "Hate Crime Statistics."

number of crimes against women (not women's property) as compared to men.[25] These statistics prove what we Black LBTQ women already know and live with: the danger of being Black and female and lesbian, bisexual, transgender, or queer.

In addition to the daily awareness of the danger of being who we are, that is, women and LBTQ, others constantly press upon our souls our lack of rights as equal citizens. We are deeply hurt when our very own people launch sexism and homophobia against us! This was the case between Pauli Murray and Bayard Rustin.

Rustin, credited with being the leading strategist of the 1963 March on Washington, was a gay Black man who wrote a scathing commentary against women's rights. For the most part Murray agreed with his criticisms, but she was disappointed that he failed to understand and address the full demands and focus of the movement. Her response conveyed her displeasure with Rustin ("Now, Bayard, would you please descend from your lofty masculine height and become a brother for a few minutes?"[26]) and addresses the sexism of Bayard and other Black men. Of the National Organization for Women (NOW), of which she was co-founder, Murray said: "The women's movement has sprung up with renewed vitality primarily because it was impossible to convince our brethren, including you, dear Bayard, that women's rights were and are an integral part of the civil rights-human rights revolution and that human rights are indivisible!"[27]

The dilemma of having a Black man deny your full and equal rights as a woman was not a matter that women took without response. Rustin's sexism apparently became well known within the women's rights movement and Murray within this same letter recounted a story relayed to her about his behavior toward several women of the Women's National Press Club.

> The story has gone the rounds that when you accepted on A. Philip Randolph's behalf the invitation to speak at the National Press Club, women members of the press came to you to plead that he not accept this invitation but instead to speak at the Women's Press Club (name not quite accurate) which does not exclude men. The National Press Club, a male organization, not only did (and probably still does) not accept women press corps for membership, but even when they were assigned to cover events there as reporters

25. FBI, "National Incident-Based Reporting System."
26. Murray, Papers, Letter to Bayard Rustin, September 9, 1970.
27. Ibid.

they were compelled to sit in the balcony. These women reportedly reminded you of this and you reportedly replied, "What's wrong with the balcony?" They retorted, "What's wrong with the back of the bus?"[28]

The most poignant part of Murray's letter to Rustin includes several "trends" of pronounced male domination within the leadership ranks of which she took note during her work with the movement. These trends are not unique to Murray; other African American female activists, such as Ella Baker, have given similar analyses of the movement.

In any movement for social justice we must take care that we do not quiet the voices of the oppressed within our community for the sake of lifting up the oppressed *de jure*. Perhaps we have learned this lesson well from the internal scuffles of the '60s civil rights movement. The hashtag message #BlackLivesMatter was created by three Black women two of whom identify as queer, Alicia Garza and Patrisse Cullors, in the wake of the trial of George Zimmerman for the killing of Trayvon Martin. By the time Michael Brown was killed, the social media hashtag had become and now is a major project and call to action against excessive police force and the racist targeting of Black bodies. Anyone who adds the hashtag #BlackLivesMatter to their Twitter or Facebook post is reminded that the Black lives that matter include Black LGBTQ lives.

Unfortunately, the healing and reconciliation that Murray longed for has not been realized, in her time nor mine. The St. Louis grand jury investigating the killing of Michael Brown decided against bringing Darren Wilson to trial. The New York grand jury decided not to try the police officer that killed Eric Garner. Businesses were set afire, looting began once again, protests are now occurring at a national level. We wait to hear what will become of the grand jury investigation into the police killing of twelve-year old Tamir Rice. The vision of paradise in which the wolf lies down with the lamb is far from becoming reality.[29] As I watch the growing rage of young adults from all racial-ethnic groups, I remain in prayer against a bitterness of our souls. May God's love coat our souls and shield our spirits so that our anger remains righteous and our protest civil and, as justice requires, disobedient.

28. Ibid.

29. From Isaiah 11:6, "The wolf shall live with the lamb, the leopard shall lie down with the kid, the calf and the lion and the fatling together, and a little child shall lead them."

CHAPTER 6

Transforming Until
Thy Kin(g)dom Come

THE CREATION STORY DECLARES that God took that which was nothingness and formed the world. The message of salvation is predicated on the central idea that God enters this temporal created space by taking on human flesh in the body of Jesus Christ. Through the incarnation God dwelled with humanity and ultimately died on a cruel cross. The doctrine of atonement teaches that the crucifixion of God's first born and only son, Jesus Christ, was foreseen and allowed to come to pass so that sinners could be reconciled to God. By the suffering, death, and resurrection of Christ we are made at one with God. We are offered salvation and eternal life when we repent of our sins and accept Christ as Savior.

Salvation transforms us from sinners to redeemed persons. It is a transformation of the soul, a transformation of our lives, and ultimately a transformation of our very being. "We will not all die, but we will all be changed," is the promise of everlasting life for the righteous, those who have received salvation.[1] The corporeal mass is transformed to spiritual imperishability. The entire Christian faith is based on these declarations of transformation whose final goal is to be in absolute union with God. We are not now what God desires, but through Christ Jesus we shall be changed and are even now being changed.

Similarly, Queer theology is interested in transformation. It challenges us to be transformed in our minds and hearts as we reconsider what we

1. 1 Corinthians 15:51

have been taught about human sexuality. It addresses our theological dispositions by encouraging us to look outside our socialized constructs of fixed sexual identity and expression. It does this by analyzing the presuppositions of our faith, by pondering our dogma and doctrine. It dares us to talk and do critical reflection about God in light of our existential situation and as we question the accepted verities of our existence.

To be sure, theology requires a certain fluidity of thought that is initiated by the willingness to suspend our beliefs so that we may pursue God's truths for our lives. *Semper Reformanda.* We are always reforming on the journey towards the Beloved Kingdom, the heavenly kingdom on earth, which is the site of union with God and, *ipso facto*, is a place where righteousness and justice will be realized. The journey, this pursuit of God's truth for our lives, means a dedication to a process of transformation for the sake of gaining the ultimate liberation of our mind, bodies and soul. Our hope is rooted in the possibility of transformation: from mortality to immortality.

Likewise transformation is the hope of transgender men and women. It is the hope of transformation in many forms: of mind, of soul, and yes, of body. While all three transformations are important, in this chapter I will discuss the latter transformation largely because I have found the transformation of gender, particularly the physical transformation of body from one recognizable gender identity to another, to be the subject not sufficiently covered within queer theology. Having spent a great deal of time reading and being in conversation with others about transgender identity and expression, it finally occurred to me one day that I needed to come to grips with how I was applying the doctrine of creation to the lived journeys of transgender people.

Admittedly, my application of the doctrine of creation was insufficient to this task because it was fixed on the point at which God "created male and female." It was stuck on the story of two bodies made, two perfect bodies at that. I did not take into account that it is in fact, *doctrine*, not fact. As doctrine, it is important to our Christian lives. For the doctrine of creation gives Black LGBTQ persons hope in that it has reminded us that our lives are not in the care of human hands but in the hands of an infinite God. This is one of the most significant functions for this doctrine as regards queer theology.

However, as doctrine it is also not irrefutable, in part or in whole. What is at issue with the doctrine of creation as it relates to the human body is whether we must hang our hat at the point of two primordial lives, insisting that the story/stories of the shaping of their bodies serve(s) as the ending of the history of human bodies being formed. We should not do so. Yet this is what we are prodded to accept each time a minister utters, "God made Adam and Eve not Adam and Steve." On the one hand we are taught and many believe that Adam was the first created human and from his body God created Eve. On the other hand, God is the sustainer of Creation. As sustainer, God continues to be the Giver of Life for each newborn child. That is, God continues to be present and a vital part of the ongoing story of Creation. Thus any theology related to the doctrine of creation is ultimately more a doctrine about the God of Creation. It is inevitably about who God is, what God has done, *and* about what God is *still* doing through humanity whom God created. God is still at work bringing God's good creation to its final goal that shall be accomplished in Jesus Christ, the goal of the kingdom of God.

God's continued work in the world through the *telos of creation*, the end of creation through the coming reign of God in Jesus Christ, is God working in mysterious ways. Just as God works in mysterious ways, so too are the ways of God's creation. The world and, yes, life is not wholly understood but much of our world and our lives remain mysteries. We know only in part.

One would think that given our advanced technology we would know everything about the human body at this point, and yet it is our greatest mystery. Even now scientists are hard at work on genetics research studying human DNA. We have bodies. We just don't fully know how they work. Neither do we always understand why our bodies do not work as they should or as we think they should. What science often does is help us to live our best lives in the bodies our souls inhabit, mystery notwithstanding.

Yet, the presumption that their birth bodies are "how God made you" has negatively affected the day-to-day living of transpersons. Some have shared with us their testimonies of knowing their bodies of birth do not match their internally understood gender. To wit, their male or female anatomies and external organs of birth may be how they were born and how the rest of the world perceives them, but their self-identity is different. For example, a person's body may have the external organs of a biological female but that person's self-identity may be male, or vice versus. Further, transgender persons' sexual orientation may be lesbian, gay, bisexual, or heterosexual. How is that? Because transgender identity is about how gender is understood and not about sexual attraction or what is known as sexual orientation. Given the increase in hate crime attacks, transpobic "how God made you" statements, and the sheer energy needed to endure bigotry while trying to survive as a whole and healthy person, the doctrine of creation rightly articulated can be an enormous theological treasure for transgender persons of faith. The question should not be "What are you?"—related to body—but "Who are you?" which shifts the conversation in the proper direction of who we are as people of God.

Unfortunately, the "how God made you" is the go-to justification some people use to denigrate and even viciously attack transpersons. It is as much a theological perspective as it is a rationale to do harm. As theology it is poorly shaped when it uses the argument of "how God made you" to discriminate and harm transpersons.

Nonetheless, the doctrine of creation as an eschatological treatment can be helpful in queer theology and specifically when reflecting on our bodily participation in the ongoing work of tending to God's created world and helping to usher in, through the activities of our bodies God's kingdom come, God's will be done. Speaking eschatologically, we are all made in the *imago dei* with our divine responsibility of helping usher in the teleological "*not yet*" while living within this present age. To do so, in each age, humanity has the right and indeed duty to live out its fullest purpose by being the most authentic and healthy selves possible. The desire for authenticity and wholeness of body and soul is, I believe, the desire of every transperson who undergoes gender transition surgery. I believe the same holds true for all transpersons. Particularly given the fact that, "not every transperson wants or can afford GRS," as my friend Monica Roberts reminded me.[2]

The story of Creation does not conclude with an emphasis on the human body but human beings in right relationship with God living in the eschatological fulfillment of a "new heaven and a new earth."[3] This New Jerusalem will be the "home of God" where God will, "dwell with them; they will be his peoples, and God himself will be with them; he will wipe every tear from their eyes. Death will be no more; mourning and crying and pain will be no more, for the first things have passed away."[4] The hope of the New Jerusalem therefore contains the promise of the end of suffer-

2. Quoted from a Facebook instant message conversation between Pamela R. Lightsey and Black transwoman Monica Roberts, November 1, 2014. "GRS" means "genital reconstruction/reassignment surgery." Here also I want to note that I use the terms "transgender persons" and "transpeople" synonymously.

3. Revelation 21:1.

4. Revelation 21:3b–4

ing for the people of God. This is what has made the doctrine of Creation such a compelling teaching for Black Americans who have endured racial oppression for centuries. It is not solely what God has done for humanity but the eschatological work of making all things new including a world where suffering is extinct that has brought us peace in the midst of crisis and hope during times of great tribulation. Black transpersons no less than Black gender conforming persons have embraced that hope while suffering the cruelty of racism and, what is more, while enduring the additional oppression of transphobia. They have participated in this work as agents of social justice and as members of the body of Christ.

The ongoing work of tending to Creation as co-laborers with Christ benefits from the support of all within that body of believers especially transpersons. I count Pauli Murray on the roll of transpersons because of her many pages of autobiographical material detailing her struggle. In one letter to her aunt, Murray takes up her aunt's acceptance of her "boy-girl" personality saying, "where you and a few people understand, the world does not accept my pattern of life. And to try to live by society's standards always causes me such inner conflict that at times it's almost unbearable."[5] Murray's most pleasurable experiences included traveling around the country dressed as a boy. Her archives contain stories of her "in drag" experience such as her travels with Peggie Holmes in 1935: "Still scared about the trip. Wondering if we're doing the right thing, Have no way of knowing yet. At least we're trying to solve our problem in the best way possible . . . Earned 25¢ in Roscoe carrying package. Lady though I was a Boy Scout. ..Long walk thru [sic] city—serious talk with Peg re P-P relationship."[6]

Though several pages in Rev. Pauli Murray's journal are reflections on her own gender identity and sexism, they also chronicle her ideas regarding the sexism of Black ministers within the Southern Christian Leadership Conference, her work as co-founder of the National Organization for Women (N.O.W.) and her intimate relationships with women. Her insistence on being called "Pauli" rather than her given name, "Anna Pauline," is indicative of Murray's understood gender identity. "Why the inverted sex instinct–wearing pants, wanting to be one of the men, doing

5. Murray, Papers, June 2, 1943, Box 10; Folder 253.

6. Murray, Papers, Saturday, April 27, 1935, through Tuesday, May 7, 1935. Box 1, Folder 25. Note: Peg is likely her longtime friend Peggie Holmes. "P-P relationship" logically refers to the relationship between Peg and Pauli.

things that fellows do, hating to be dominated by women unless I like them?–Answer–glandular."[7]

Identifying as a feminist, Murray's transcript of an interview with Robert Martin of *East Village* details the burgeoning feminist discourse of her time as well as her frustration with exclusionist practices against her by Black clergy and young Black nationalists. Of being identified as feminist, Murray responded:

> But I am a feminist only in the same way that I am a Negroist [sic]; I am really neither–I'm a humanist. I believe that human rights are indivisible and so, wherever a human right is denied I become an 'ist' for the group. So I'm a feminist because women have been denied their rights and because I would be disloyal to my own sex, if I did not fight for women's rights. And I will not let my black brothers divide me up and say that one part of me must take priority over the other part. Unlike Negro men, I have the double problem of fighting for both aspects of my personality.[8]

Murray's work is an inspiring resource for Queer womanist theology. It prompts us to take seriously the eradication of suffering enforced by bodily limitations. If indeed "the first things have passed away"[9] in the New Jerusalem, and if there will be no more suffering, then the eschatological vision of the liberation of the oppressed, to include LGBTQ persons, will only reach fruition when justice "roll[s] down like waters, and righteousness like an ever-flowing stream."[10] The vitality of theology can be gauged by its capacity to address righteousness as the fundamental premise of God's eschatological promise.

Queering the doctrine of creation is therefore especially needful for gender nonconforming persons. It reminds us of God's loving work for our total being, that what God called "good" includes all living beings. The continued presence of God in the world, especially God's providential care of this world, is not exclusive but inclusive of people from all walks of life. As our nation sees with new eyes the beauty of the presence and work of LGBTQ persons it is really playing catch up to what we who refused to give up our faith have always known and insisted upon: God loves us.

7. Murray, Papers, December 16, 1937, Box 4, Folder 71

8. Murray, Papers, August 16, 1968, Box 1, Folder 7.

9. Revelation 21:4.

10. Amos 5:24.

While not everyone accepts that statement, change is happening. One of the most popular Black transwomen of our time is Laverne Cox of the television series, *Orange is The New Black*. An icon among Black LBTQ women, she has helped transform the way many in America thinks about transgender persons. The first openly transperson nominated for an Emmy and NAACP Image Award, Cox delivered a stunning portrayal of the challenges of transpersons within the penal system, even taking on the subject of access to post-surgery hormone treatments. Appearing on the cover of TIME magazine, Ms. Cox drew readers to her story of womanhood in Mobile, Alabama, coming out to family, and her insistence that, "There's not just one trans story. There's not just one trans experience."[11]

What this means is that though some persons have chosen to have sex reassignment/affirmation surgery, not all choose or can afford the preoperative preparatory treatments and/or surgery. One is not transgender as a matter of surgery but as a matter of self-understanding. As Janet Mock states, "A trans person can be straight, gay, bisexual, etc.; a cis gay, lesbian, or heterosexual person can conform to expected gender norms or not; and a woman can have a penis and a man can have a vagina. There is no formula when it comes to gender and sexuality."[12]

The Creation story, what God has done and what God is doing for and in the world, never posits a singular way of being human or insists that only one type human is acceptable. What is most important in the early stories and what holds our interest is how we inhabit this world. Among God's first disappointment with humanity is the story of one brother killing another brother, Cain and Abel. More than our bodily parts, more than our offered gifts to God, we are required to love and care for one another. The lesson of Creation is therefore also a lesson of learning to be in right relationship with one another.

As we reflect upon the doctrine of Creation we must keep in mind not only the relationship between Adam and Eve, but between all who have come thereafter. Taking into account the lived reality and hopes of transwomen of color, we must face the disproportionate number of transwomen of color who are victims of hate crimes. "More than half [72%] of 2013's homicide victims were transgender women of color . . . Black and African American survivors were two times as likely to experience discrimination

---

11. Steinmetz, "Laverne Cox Talks to TIME about the Transgender Movement."

12. Mock, *Redefining Realness*, 50.

compared to overall survivors."[13] These statistics reveal that race is an important variable in hate crimes against transgender women. It also reveals that Black transwomen are in a state of crisis across our nation. African American transwoman activist, Monica Roberts, responded to the violent attack of an African American transwoman who was stabbed forty times by saying,

> I'm quite aware that in the coming days the majority within the minority, may say I lost my marbles, but WTF! My sisters, black trans women, continue to be disproportionately impacted by violence and hate crimes, while others continue to enjoy privilege. It is true that trans people as a whole have had some monumental wins lately but damn, we're talking the difference between not being harassed or imprisoned while peeing and getting stabbed, shot, or murdered before even making it to the bathroom. Black Trans women—African American Trans Women—are getting slaughtered.[14]

Hate crime perpetrators target Black transwomen because they are Black and because they do not conform to heteronormative ideals. To be Black and transwoman means being vulnerable on a day-to-day basis. We must address factors like transphobia, religious fundamentalism, and racism in order to end the killing of these innocent women. This is why it is vital that we turn a critical eye to the history of discrimination against Black transwomen and that we also pay attention to the lives and history of Black transwomen whose work and lives remind us of the many sacrifices made so that nongenderconforming women can enjoy the privileges of the day.

Nearly lost in the chronicles of Black history is the story of one transwoman who did just that: Georgia Black. Perhaps I should not say, "nearly lost" because her story is well known by many Black LBTQ women. I lift her story up in this work with the hopes that her life will be honored well beyond our Black LBTQ community.

13. Insert mine. Stats taken from: *NVAVP Report: 2012 Lesbian, Gay, Bisexual, Transgender, Queer and HIV-Affected Hate Violence in 2012.* "The overwhelming majority of homicide victims (78%) were Black and African American, 11% of homicide victims were Latin@, and 11% of homicide victims were White. More than half (72%) of victims were transgender women, while 67% of homicide victims were transgender women of color."

14. Monica Roberts, "DC Trans Woman Stabbed 40 Times in Attack," *TransGriot Blog,* June 25, 2013, http://transgriot.blogspot.com/2013/06/dc-trans-woman-stabbed-40-times-in.html.

The story of Georgia Black originally appeared in *Ebony Magazine* in October 1951 and was reprinted for their thirtieth anniversary edition in November 1975. Mrs. Black's story is strangely enough included in an issue that contains an article written by Eleanor Roosevelt entitled, "Some of My Best Friends are Negro." Mrs. Roosevelt chronicles her several Negro friendships including with Mary McLeod Bethune and Pauli Murray.[15] As if to bookmark the "hot topic" the editors presented, this issue's reader comment section dealt largely with responses to an article in a previous issue that dealt with interracial marriages.

I doubt that the editors of *Ebony* knew of the several relationships with women Mrs. Roosevelt is now rumored to have enjoyed. The honor of having an article penned by the First Lady of the United States was great and unprecedented for the civil rights movement. The irony of First Lady Roosevelt writing about her "Negro friends" while neither she nor Dr. Murray could speak publicly nor live out their lives according to how they self-identified sexually is strikingly apparent nowadays. This article's reprinting in *Ebony*, known as the leading magazine of the Black community, along with republication of the story of Georgia Black, seems almost an invitation to analysis. At the very least, the two articles invite contemporary readers, especially LGBTQ persons like myself, to remember and honor the lives of queer women who have made it possible for us to live our lives in sync with our self-understood gender.

The article most relevant to this work, "The Man Who Lived 30 Years as A Woman," details–though not nearly enough–the phenomenal life of Georgia Black. This gutsy woman decided at the age of fifteen to spend her life as the gender that accurately expressed her self-awareness.[16] Married twice and the adopted mother of one son, Georgia's death was received with great sorrow. "Negro and white mourners rubbed elbows, bowed heads and shed genuine tears" at her funeral cortege.[17] Prior to her death, her pastor, Rev. Joseph Williams was photographed shaking hands with members who congratulated him regarding his sermon in which he asked for prayers for Sis. Georgia Black.[18] Speaking about her self-understanding, "Georgia insisted that fate had intended him to be female. Admitting that he had male

15. Roosevelt, "Some of My Best Friends are Negro," 73–78.

16. *Ebony Magazine*, "Man Who Lived Thirty Years as a Woman," 85.

17. Ibid.

18. Ibid., 86.

organs, he dismissed them as "'growths.'"[19] There is no medical evidence that points to Georgia's "growths" as actually being signs that she was intersex and therefore I count her narrative among the several narratives of Black trans rather than intersexed women.[20]

Georgia adapted her day-to-day living so that her gender identity and expression was as she self-identified, exquisitely woman. Housewife, mother, and respected community member, I am highlighting Georgia's life because unlike some in our day who have walked away from the church this Christian woman was a faithful church member and leader of the Women's Missionary Society.[21] Pictured with members of her church, the article states, "Black, who owned rooming house, often used home to raise fund to support church." Rather than condemn Mrs. Black, "Sanford public opinion was divided into two classes: those who didn't believe Black had deceived them and those who didn't care."[22] Though Ms. Black might have suffered some level of isolation, we know that she was beloved within the fellowship of believers and chose to remain within the church rather than walk away having nothing to do with organized religion.

Today there are many LGBTQ-affirming churches that transgender people of faith regularly attend. Unfortunately, predominately Black LGBTQ-affirming churches remain few in number. It is easy enough for us who are Black to talk about liberation but when it comes to the liberation of Black people who are a minority within this minority the conversation very often turns to irrational babble. We want justice within our lives and within our churches but have not yet been willing to say with a full majority voice that justice within the church should be extended to every member. Ironically, we resist the very changes that will bring justice, even as we long for change.

19. Ibid., 88.

20. The Intersex Society of North America explains the term "intersex" in this way: "'Intersex' is a general term used for a variety of conditions in which a person is born with a reproductive or sexual anatomy that doesn't seem to fit the typical definitions of female or male. For example, a person might be born appearing to be female on the outside, but having mostly male-typical anatomy on the inside. Or a person may be born with genitals that seem to be in-between the usual male and female types—for example, a girl may be born with a noticeably large clitoris, or lacking a vaginal opening, or a boy may be born with a notably small penis, or with a scrotum that is divided so that it has formed more like labia. Or a person may be born with mosaic genetics, so that some of her cells have XX chromosomes and some of them have XY."

21. *Ebony Magazine*, "Man Who Lived Thirty Years as a Woman," 85.

22. Ibid., 88.

Getting to that point of total liberation will mean the eradication of discrimination based on sexual identity as well as race. Each season of the transformation of our churches is fraught with its own challenges and pain. However, just as we have seen progress related to the LGBQ movement in our Black churches and community, we must be even more diligent to ensure our march toward justice finds us in solidarity with our trans brothers and sisters, especially our Black transwomen who have been the disproportionate victims of attacks especially within the Black community. We must not be comfortable or accept any notion of having crossed "over into the promised land" if our trans sisters are still raising the funds without receiving the earned interest of being benefactors to our liberation.

As children of God and part of this expansive Creation, we must all be free to live and to worship God without fear of physical and psychological retaliation. God is still at work, in and through each of us. Therefore we must remain co-caretakers of that good and coming kin-dom of God, honoring *the imago dei* present in each of our lives.

CHAPTER 7

Imago Dei

We Flesh That Needs Lovin'

"Here," she said, "in this here place, we flesh; flesh that weeps, laughs; flesh that dances on bare feet in grass. Love it. Love it hard. Yonder they do not love your flesh. They despise it . . . *You* got to love it. This is flesh I'm talking about here. Flesh that needs to be loved. Feet that need to rest and to dance; backs that need support; shoulders that need arms, strong arms I'm telling you. And oh my people, out yonder, hear me, they do not love your neck unnoosed and straight. So love your neck; put a hand on it, grace it, stroke it, and hold it up. And all your inside parts that they'd just as soon slop for hogs, you got to love them. The dark, dark liver—love it, love it, and the beat and beating heart, love that too. More than eyes or feet . . . More than your life-holding womb and your live-giving private parts, hear me now, love your heart. For this is the prize."[1]

IN 1998, I WAS touched deeply by a scene in the movie, *Beloved*, based on Toni Morrison's novel of the same name. The scene is located in a place called the Clearing; a place known only by the Black people of Cincinnati. Sitting there, surrounded by the many who gathered every Saturday, Baby Suggs, an "unchurched preacher" and mother-in-law of the protagonist Sethe, powerfully exhorts the people to love their flesh.

The symbolism of naming this location "Clearing," would not be lost on those who read the novel. It is not simply "a wide-open place cut deep

1. Morrison, *Beloved*, 104–5.

in the woods."[2] It is most importantly a location where the oppressed have the opportunity, if only for a little while, to *clear themselves*–mind, body, and spirit–from the constraints and bigotry they bear daily. Though Sugg does "open her great heart" in the Independent Black churches, such as the AME, Baptist and Holiness churches,[3] Morrison only details in full length this exhortation, and though she describes Sugg as an "unchurched preacher," never once does Morrison say she is preaching. In fact, "she did not tell them to clean up their lives or to go sin no more," as would be typical of preaching. Instead she spoke of grace, not in what could be seen, but only in what could be imagined.[4]

Like Morrison's character Sugg, womanists have given much attention to the value of Black bodies, especially Black women's bodies. Womanist practical theologian and psychotherapist, Phillis Sheppard, makes this argument:

> We need to consider "the body" in the context of a society where certain bodies are exploited to create a desire for commodities regardless of the need or ability to afford them; where the color of our skin continues to greatly influence our quality of life, our experiences in society, and our economic locations . . . where sex and sexuality are used to sell "entertainment" infused with violence. We need to hear what the body has to tell us about being created in the image of God.[5]

In this chapter, I will take up Baby Sugg's and Dr. Sheppard's challenge in order to hear what the bodies of Black LBTQ women tell us about being made in God's likeness and image and to imagine the good that can be realized if we take seriously the gift of God's gracious act. My overarching goal is to make the case that the sacred worth of lesbians, gays, bisexual, transgender, and queer person as currently connected to the doctrine of *imago Dei*[6] has no currency with queer womanists when it is part of a

---

2. Ibid., 103.

3. Ibid.

4. Ibid., 104.

5. Sheppard, *Self, Culture and Others in Womanist Practical Theology*, 145.

6. The concept that, like Adam, all humanity is created in the image of God implies the inherent value/worth of all people. That original image with associated "good and perfect traits" was marred by the sin of Adam, and only through salvation are we given the possibility of being daily "renewed" to our original, authentic state. Nonetheless, within every human being is some measure of God's likeness.

denominational polity that at the same time prohibits sexual relations by monogamous same-sex spouses and between same-sex couples.

To unpack this doctrine of the Church we start with scripture, Genesis 1: 26:

> Then God said, "Let us make (נַעֲשֶׂה na·ʿă·śeh / asah—accomplish) humankind in our image (בְּצַלְמֵנוּ bə·ṣal·mê·nū / tselem—in our image), according to our likeness (תּוּמָד demuth / kiḏ·mū·ṯê·nū—in our likeness) . . ."

Nothing of the precise nature or material traits of image צֶלֶם and likeness תּוּמָד of God is recorded. The only other reference we have to this act is in verse 31:

> God saw everything that he had made (הָשָׂה ʿā·śāh / asah—accomplish) and, indeed it was very good (בוֹט ṭō·wḇ / towb—good).

The commonly held interpretation of this text addressing the story of Creation is that God made the first people in a way that closely resembled God's own self. The doctrine purports that humanity, both man and woman, were made in God's image, and given the responsibility to care for Earth and all its animals and vegetation. It points to the text's description of the relationship God intended between the two humans and between the humans and the rest of Creation including the planet. This understanding and concept known as *imago Dei* is an ancient doctrine of the universal Church that we Christians have inherited by Holy Tradition and maintained by divine revelation and study of scripture. It is particularly relevant to queer womanist theology that contains as its fundamental tenet the idea of fluid relationality between humanity, God, and Creation. We suggest it is fluid because of the imagery of interconnected and unconstrained relationships with one another, God and Creation. We take seriously what womanist ethicist, Marcia Riggs said of the doctrine:

> The *imago Dei* in each of us must not be relegated to something essentially human nor to a way of relating to one another that is contingent on our ability to transcend or ignore our bodily differences. We, in all our embodied differences, incarnate the *imago Dei*.[7]

Riggs reminds us of the divinely created gift of diversity through our bodily differences and that the *imago Dei* within each of us brings universality

---

7. Riggs, "Living as Religious Ethical Mediators," 250.

into our particularities. To wit, the *imago Dei* is a daily reminder of the interconnectedness of life. Through the gift of *imago Dei*, God is both transcendentally and immanently in relationship with humanity. Both beyond and with. Through the acts of tselem and demuth–held together–as with Holy Conception, God comes out.

The action of *image and likeness making* is not a complete revelation, but like our own coming out, it marks the journey of origins. Creation was that time when we were totally naked with one another, completely intimate with ourselves, each other, and before our God. That was the state of original complete satisfaction. Our task, as people made in the image and likeness of God, is to overcome the persistent temptation not to love and appreciate what God has called good. That temptation is what the early Church Fathers and Mothers considered inordinate self-love. On the other hand, because Black women's bodies and queer bodies historically have been the site of abuse and powerlessness, we must not embrace any theology of *imago Dei* that does not contain a commitment to nurture appropriate self-love. In the paragraphs to come, I will elucidate the value of having this two-pronged task.

Queer womanist theologians must be vigilant that our interpretation of the doctrine of *imago Dei* properly articulates the pitfalls of unhealthy self-love. Inordinate self-love is what Augustine had in mind when he spoke of pride or "craving for undue exaltation"[8] as the basic form of sin. Here the concern is that we not develop a sense of our own selves that lacks humility before God and the inability to interact respectfully with others. This craving for exaltation hinders our ability to become our best selves and instead of being life giving, leads us on the path of destruction.

Theologian Reinhold Niebuhr offered a brilliant contemporary theological analysis of four theological references including pride and sin that have been the primordial enemy of our ability to recognize our highest potential in Creation and in relationship with God. I discuss Niebuhr's work in depth because of the deleterious use of the four concepts, including sex and sensuality, against LGBTQ persons.

In his masterful work, *The Nature and Destiny of Man*, Niebuhr chronicles the origin of pride to the event of Creation. Over and against the classic understanding of pride as rebellion against God, for Niebuhr pride is occasioned by humanity's sense of finiteness as "contingent existence." He describes the descent in this way: "Man falls into pride, when

8. Augustine, *City of God* 19.13 (Dods, 2:25).

he seeks to raise his contingent existence to unconditioned significance; he falls into sensuality, when he seeks to escape from his unlimited possibilities of freedom, from the perils and responsibilities of self-determination, by immersing himself into a "mutable good," by losing himself into some natural vitality."[9]

According to Niebuhr, anxiety is the antecedent to the fall of humanity. It begins when we realize our own finitude and seek to resolve that anxiety by blindly using the gift of freedom to create our own bondage. Anxiety prevents humanity from accurately interpreting God's gracious acts of creation and "unlimited possibilities of freedom." Then cometh pride and ultimately sin. Pride is the basic component of sin. It is the unwillingness to accept the finiteness of one's existence. Once victim to pride, humanity falls prey to *sensuality* that is described by Niebuhr: "Sensuality is, in effect, the inordinate love for all creaturely and mutable values which results from the primal love of self, rather than love of God."[10]

What Niebuhr best offers for this writing is his critique of the effort to regard sex as sinful. Because sensuality for Niebuhr was *inordinate love* it could, though not necessarily, find expression in the act of sex.

> The real situation is that man, granted his "fallen" nature, sins in his sex life but not because sex is essentially sinful. Or in other words, man, having lost the true centre of his life in God, falls into sensuality; and sex is the most obvious occasion for the expression of sensuality and the most vivid expression of it. Thus sex reveals sensuality to be the first and final form of self-love, secondly an effort to escape self-love by the deification of another and finally as an escape from the futilities of both forms of idolatry by a plunge into unconsciousness.[11]

Sex is not inherently or, as Niebuhr puts it, "essentially" sinful. It is sinful as an expression of sensuality, which Niebuhr summarizes as: "(1) an extension of self-love to the point where it defeats its own ends; (2) an effort to escape the prison house of self by finding a god in a process or person outside the self; and (3) finally an effort to escape from the confusion: which sin has created into some form of subconscious existence."[12]

9. Niebuhr, *Nature and Destiny of Man*, 186.

10. Ibid., 232.

11. Ibid., 239.

12. Ibid., 240.

Though our present understanding of sensuality may differ from Niebuhr, the body-soul dualism that exists in the theologies of our faith traditions so rigidly guards against sensuality and by association sexuality that it results in deprecating language and hostile situations especially when related to lesbians, gays, bisexual, and transgender people. Is there a way to honor the *imago Dei*, without falling into the kind of self-love that Niebuhr describes? Is it possible to have self-love that is not self-defeating, idolatrous, or an act of escapism? Yes. But to do so we must recapture an understanding of the body as good and not evil. We must remember that flesh is not essentially evil but became/becomes sinful as it yields to the temptation to place its desires above the Creator. "But one is *tempted* by one's own desire, being lured and enticed by it; then, when that *desire* has conceived, *it gives birth to sin*, and that sin, when it is fully grown, gives birth to death."[13] [emphasis mine]

Our fleshly bodies frankly require a healthy self-love in order to come into right relationship with God and others. We ought to love our bodies—our raw, naked bodies uninhibited by the attachments of context or status!

Admittedly, this is a difficult thing to do because we are continuously bombarded by messages that tell us to love our bodies based on things derived from inordinate affections. Love our bodies only if they can move us or stand in sexy ways; love our bodies only if they can be or if they are outfitted to represent a certain status quo; love our body parts only if they conform to what is understood as physically fit. Additionally, Black LBTQ women face the steady stream of messages that tell us we cannot love our bodies because they "*look too*" unlike this or that normative standard. Enough.

It is precisely because Black women's bodies have, as Sheppard claims, "become the scapegoats for internalized black body ambivalence" that we must turn the tables, declare our bodies to be good, and encourage healthy self-love. We must do this with a sense of urgency because we have the propensity to express scapegoating in criminal activity specifically in hate crime attacks against transwomen of color. So, not only must we love ourselves but that love of self must also extend to *loving thy neighbor as thyself.* This is why the communal nature of womanism is so critical. We must love the folk, be with the folk, and not live our lives as separatists or staunch advocates of other-worldliness.

---

13. James 1:14–15.

Returning to the primordial context of humanity, one sees the profound efficaciousness of bodily relationality. Womanist are not separatist except to give time for bodily healing. As temples of the image of God, Queer womanist theology makes the claim that those bodies of LGBTQ persons are important for the task of helping build a peaceable and just world. That happens in relationships. From cross dresser Cathay Williams (aka William Cathay), the first Black woman to serve in the Army, Texas State senator Barbara Jordan, science fiction novelist Octavia Butler, and activist Angela Davis, our presence in the world matters!

Black queer women's bodies as the image of God have been the sites of unconditional love. With our hands we have cared for the sick. With our mouths we have spoken courageous words of justice such as Sojourner Truth's message to men on women's rights: "You have been having our rights for so long, that you think, like a slaveholder, that you own us."[14]

Psychotherapist Abraham Maslow in his article, *A Theory of Motivation*, which is his explication of Kurt Goldstein's concept of self-actualization, helpfully suggests that: "Love and affection, as well as their possible expression in sexuality, are generally looked upon with ambivalence and are customarily hedged about with many restrictions and inhibitions. Theorists of psychopathology have stressed *thwarting of the love needs as basic in the picture of maladjustment*. [Emphasis mine.] Many clinical studies have therefore been made of this need and we know more about it perhaps than any of the other needs except the physiological ones."[15] Without loving relationships we are not whole.

In making the case for a *hierarchy of needs* Maslow suggests *love needs* are "friends, or a sweetheart, or a wife, or children . . . affectionate relations with people in general."[16] Though Maslow was careful to insist on defining love as "not synonymous with sex," love expressed through sex with a "sweetheart or wife" has long been regarded as healthy emotional behavior whereas the lack of sex in these relationships–except when mutually agreed or physiologically impossible–is unhealthy.

However, Sheppard has given a caution about African American women's bodies that is worth noting: "our bodies must assume an

14. Truth,"When Women Gets Her Rights Man Will Be Right," 38.

15. Maslow, "Theory of Motivation," 370–96. This is an inclusive version of Maslow's famous quotation, "What a man can be, he must be. This need we may call self-actualization."

16. Ibid.

epistemological status without reducing 'experience' to the body."[17] In other words Sheppard is saying that we must be able to speak of what we know of our bodies without making our existential situations, our experiences, the primary and/or sole subject about our bodies. Note she does not suggest our bodily experiences are not at all worthy of investigation. However, while being able to be in affectionate relations is of utmost value—an experience—we should not elevate our bodily expressions over our bodily worth. Both are critical and both require our attention.

Only when we can imagine our bodies fashioned as good rather than only in terms of sexual acts will we be able to usher in a healthy discussion on the sacred worth of queer bodies. Attaching to our conversations a myopic evaluation of LGBTQ persons as sacred but also sinful—if they fulfill their bodily needs for intimacy—is oppressive and an unhealthy restriction. While we do not fully understand sexuality, we do know sex is a human drive. To my thinking, this has not been a point of disagreement in our current church discussions.

Having said that, let me make the bold declaration that any church or denomination having established, as in the case of The United Methodist Church, that "all persons are individuals of sacred worth, created in the image of God,"[18] behaves disingenuously when it prohibits those very persons from living in ways consistent with the varied expressions of what it means to be a loving human being, not the least of which is sex. The prohibition is simply evidence of a lack of faith and an example of the will to control.

As a young woman, I was a member of the Church of God, Cleveland, Tennessee. One of the commitments of this denomination was for divine order in the home. We were taught that the husband was head of the household; a woman must be obedient to her husband; and the husband must honor the woman because she is the weaker sex. In practice, this theological interpretation of scripture was demonstrated in an attitude about women as subordinate to men and in its worst use, in abusive sexual expression. It sprang from an antiquated understanding of the human body and human sexuality, especially that women were frail physically and in their sexual expression. The current dominatrix character or the one who is a "woman on the streets and a freak in the sheets," though appreciated in our conversations, was not given the character church hierarchy used in its teaching about the "place of women." Though women could be ordained,

17. Sheppard, *Self, Culture and Others in Womanist Practical Theology,* 148.
18. *Book of Discipline of The United Methodist,* ¶161.

even as clergy, their bodies were nonetheless the sites of control by church hierarchy.

It should be no wonder that queer lesbian womanist scholars refuse to sit idly by without protesting current denominational restrictions on the body based on faulty use of theological sources to address human sexuality. With the benefit of history, we remind the Church that it was not long ago that we were denied the sacraments and rites of the Church because our bodies were deemed inhuman.

Slave masters controlled when Black bodies rested and when they were made to work; controlled when we reproduced and with whom we would have sex; controlled when and whether we could marry, receive communion, or be baptized.

Some say the current LGBTQ protest against the Church is misguided because it is based upon foundations of civil protest and that we ought not wage a protest against the Church in order to secure the entitled rites of membership. "Rights," they say, "are not rites." Queer womanists remind the Church that the administration of the sacred rites is our right of membership and this is not the first time in the history of the church that persons have made these claims on the basis of "rights" as a class of people.

Currently, The United Methodist Church has some of the most oppressive policies against same-sex loving people. Some pastors have even gone so far as to deny membership to lesbian and gay persons who refuse to denounce their sexuality and declare it as a "sin" to be "saved from." These pastors (and many members) see it as their Christian duty to help "save the sin sick soul from hell." Failing to insist on what they consider "holy standards" would be tantamount to disobeying God and letting the church "go to hell in a handbasket."

However, LGBTQ persons countered this argument. If the church's desire is to continue to refuse the full membership rites and benefits of the rituals of the church to LGBTQ persons that they extend to all other members, then the church ought to withhold the baptismal rites to every child born into its fold because the denomination has no intention to allow the members of the church to live out fully the vows it promises on that day and this declaration:

> With God's help we will proclaim the good news and live according to the example of Christ. We will surround these persons with a community of love and forgiveness, that they may grow in their trust of God, and be found faithful in their service to others. We

will pray for them, that they may be true disciples who walk in the way that leads to life.[19]

It was not too long ago that white slaveholders (many Methodists) not only refused to allow many slaves to marry, but they did so with the rationalization that as chattel property slaves had no rights to the rituals of the Church. Women for some time were not allowed the same rights to ordination as their male counterparts because women were considered subordinate to men and to allow women to become preachers was considered to be in direct defiance of scripture. But the lowest denial of the rites of the Church that we say little about is the denial of the baptismal rites to slaves. Unlike allowing marriage, which many Protestants did not recognize as a sacrament, the baptismal and Eucharist rites are sacraments of Protestant and Catholic churches alike. Because baptism is conferred upon those who accept Christ,[20] for a time many slaveholders refused to allow baptism of their slaves, primarily because they were not considered humans but brutish animals and therefore ineligible for baptism, and secondarily because they feared that the act of baptism made slaves free. "Repeatedly, would-be-missionaries to the slaves complained that slaveholders refused them permission to catechize the slaves because baptism made it necessary to free them."[21]

Considered to be mere "brutes," Africans were sold into slavery, their bodies forced into servitude. One bishop described the colonists as having "an irrational contempt for Blacks as creatures of another species, who had no right to be instructed or admitted to the sacraments; have proved a main obstacle to the conversion of these poor people."[22]

Thus just as baptizing slaves was tacit approval of their humanity, the many United Methodist Church's delegates' objection to allowing full membership and ordination privileges of LGBTQ persons has often to do with an objection related to our bodies: they perceive us either as being the embodiment of sin or as "practicing" sin with our bodies.

LGBTQ persons hoping for justice within the UMC and other Christian traditions continue to stand firmly against this line of thinking. Moreover, we refuse to allow the church to exert coercive tactics to control our

19. *Book of Worship of the United Methodist Church.*

20. Believers baptism is not practiced in the United Methodist Church. Infants are baptized. It is an act of faith regarding what God shall do in the child's life.

21. Raboteau, *Slave Religion,* 98.

22 Ibid., 100.

bodies and the decisions we make to express ourselves in loving relationships. We are not asking for an inclusion without boundaries. We know that inclusion is made possible by love and therefore when we say "All" it should not be misinterpreted to mean we endorse an "anything goes" community as is feared by some. The LGBTQ community like all people of goodwill does not advocate abuse, violence or criminal activity. We do categorically say that the framing of the argument against inclusivity in this way moves the conversation in the wrong direction emphasizing once again the "lifestyle" stereotype. We strive for full inclusion as people who love the LORD, who "practice" loving other people as persons of "sacred worth" seeking to love our neighbors as ourselves.

Full inclusion is the womanist way. Exclusion and individualism separate us from one another and Divine Love. Queer womanist work is to be attentive to the weaknesses of an idealized heavenly community made possible solely by human enterprise. We must push back against this as it breeds a sort of hegemonic insistence on universality over particularity. Queer womanist theology is a commitment to whole people existing in the wholeness of their given bodies; free bodies, sensual and spiritual in nature. The womanist way of attending to the "wholeness of entire people" presupposes inclusion and influences the type of community growth that can help the Christian church avoid the destruction too many of its adherents think is drawing nigh.

Epilogue

I COMPLETED THIS BOOK during a time of great national crisis. The killings of unarmed Black men, women, and children by police officers reached a tipping point with the killing of eighteen-year-old Ferguson resident, Michael Brown. Others, like Trayvon Martin, Aiyana Jones, Yvette Smith, Kimani Gray, Amadou Diallo, and Sean Bell, had caused a collective sigh within the African American community, but the smartphone video image of Big Mike's body lying for four-and-a-half hours in the middle of a Missouri road on a hot summer day was more than most could bear. To add insult to injury, Ferguson police officers brought dogs out to the site of the shooting, a clear "no-no" for anyone with modicum of knowledge of Black history. Complaints were also made that police allowed their dogs to urinate on the memorial.[1] These actions, plus the refusal to divulge the name of the officer who killed Michael Brown, precipitated a night of looting and weeks of protest.

As a veteran, and as the mother of a Black man who served in Iraq, I cannot adequately explain the feeling of outrage and despair that overwhelmed my heart as I watched the buildup of militarized police presence in Ferguson. Police in riot gear supported by police using BearCat armored vehicles, the LRAD Sound Cannon, camouflage clothing and boots, high power rifles, and tear gas did not lead to ending the civil unrest in Ferguson but further agitated the crowd of largely peaceful protestors. For nights I stayed up following storyline after storyline. I Googled "Ferguson" to find livestream events so that I could watch the events happening live after the national media such as CNN, MSNBC, and yes, Fox began taped repeats of programming.

---

1. Follman, "Michael Brown's Mom Laid Flowers Where He Was Shot—And Police Crushed Them."

At some point it occurred to me what I was doing: the same thing I had done when my son was in Iraq. Television on 24/7, lack of sleep, fearing another death. I experienced this as war being waged against Black citizens. As an African American, I experienced the crisis on a very personal level. August 17th after watching a church rally in honor of Michael Brown protest, I lay down for what would be my first full night of sleep since the day Brown was killed. I woke up the next day to news that the police had used tear gas on protestors and that the governor ordered the National Guard to deploy in Ferguson. After weeks of being a long distance ally, I too felt a sense of deployment but mine was a call by God to my skills as scholar and activist to dig out and show the events happening in Ferguson that were not being told by national media.

I decided to capture, as somewhat of an amateur journalist, the inner conversations and actions of Black people working to achieve justice in Ferguson. My deepest concern was that this history was being interpreted to satiate an audience accustomed to "reality-tv" and salacious headline news. I wanted to broadcast and record the events as they took place to counter the steady stream of sensationalized breaking news and misinformation. By August 19th I was on a plane to Ferguson to march in solidarity with that community. As a womanist theologian I knew one of my tasks was to work to improve the quality of life for Black people in Ferguson. Because I had longed for more livestream productions to keep up with what was happening on the ground in Ferguson, I decided to use that same technology for my work. I had the good fortune to by supported by funding from Boston University School of Theology and Reconciling Ministries Network, the latter sending two of its communications staff, Andy Oliver and M Barclay to be on the ground with me my first two days in Ferguson.

The narratives and passionate exchanges of Black women protesting in Ferguson often brought me to tears. Nothing prepares you to hear Black women screaming at police, "Stop killing our children. We love our children just like you. We carry them for 9 months just like your wives. We'll die before we let you kill another one of our children!"[2] With a look of futility one young protestor responded to my question about justice saying, "We don't even know what justice looks like!" Many protestors thank me for being on the streets marching within the ranks as one of them rather than filming from an outside parameter or interviewing from the safety of

2. Words spoken by an unknown protestor in front of Ferguson Police Department during the National March on Ferguson, August 30, 2014. Captured on livestream.

a media tent. Some expressed concern that the nation would forget their plight once major news stations moved on to the next big story. Knowledge about Ferguson and the possibility that this knowledge will be deconstructed in ways that nullify both the reasons for the protest and the protest itself has been of utmost importance to this small community.

I trained the lens of my iPhone on the women leading the protest to ensure their work is not excluded in the social production of knowledge about Ferguson. I interviewed Black queer women who were also leaders within the movement for the same reason. In fact, seeing the presence of old school patriarchy at work in some segments of the movement was not surprising. It only strengthened my resolve to show the nuances of thought and practice among Black protestors. Our complete freedom can only occur as we also free ourselves from intracultural oppression. What I have witnessed in Ferguson and the several reality programs about Black Lives is the unfortunate ongoing struggle against sexism. As a theologian, it is interesting that not only a good number of Black male clergy and Black females continue to believe that only men are capable of being leaders good leaders and especially leaders "over women." Rubbish.

I have made several trips to Ferguson since summer 2014. I have marched for justice for Michael Brown, against systemic racism, against the lapse in justice for Black people, to make this nation a better place for all Black people and by extension all Americans.

Asking for justice for Michael Brown has proven to be a divisive issue. Our desire was that the officer who killed Michael Brown be made to stand before the courts under the same "rule of law" that the predominantly white supporters of the officer who killed Brown demand that Black people accept. They can neither imagine the magnitude of our pain nor do they care. "The rule of law should be respected," they say. Yet they balk at Officer Darren Wilson being made to stand in court, innocent until proven guilty, under that same rule of law. They see no injustice in the quick demonization of Michael Brown. They believe without question police officer Darren Wilson's account as told by an anonymous friend. They find no fault in Ferguson police releasing a video showing Brown allegedly robbing a convenience store. They say Michael Brown was guilty of stealing cigarillos, though by the "rule of law" Michael Brown was never arrested on this charge nor brought to trial. They say that had Brown not resisted arrest, he would be alive today.

But then we have the case of Eric Garner. America has seen video footage of Garner pleading for his life as he is being choked to death. Despite this footage, the routine is the same: demonize the dead man, blame him for his own death, reinterpret what witnesses have seen with their own eyes,[3] valorize the officer who had the misfortune of having to "bring down" a big Black man.

In both cases, the grand jury decided not to indict the police officer. In both cases the problem is much bigger than one police officer.

It is simply not true that Black people do not value or respect police officers. I am old enough to remember civil rights leaders demanding more Black men be recruited to become police officers because we believed their presence in our communities would mean fairer treated of Black citizens. We have been stunned, on a national level to learn that Ferguson Police Department had only three Black officers.

This knowledge only justifies our critique that the problem in Ferguson and indeed with policing in America is rooted in systemic racism. The dismal recruitment record of Black police officers and the aggressive police tactics are indicative of a system that does not understand Black culture nor respect Black lives. Though having Black officers does not ensure fair treatment with each encounter, the lack of Black police presence in predominately Black communities seems nothing more than a recipe for charges of racial profiling, police brutality and increased community hostility against police.

I'm sure some readers will wonder why I did not address violent crimes that Black people commit against one another. The answer is simple: The rate of Black crimes against other Black people[4] is not causal to the killing of unarmed Blacks by police officers except to the extent that it is part of the national stereotyping that casts Black men as incorrigible criminals. Therefore, I have kept the focus of my analysis of the crisis in Ferguson on systemic racism.

The other matter activists in Ferguson and New York have drawn attention to is that our criminal justice system is capable of short-circuiting the quest for truth because we lack special prosecutors heading investigations when there is the possibility that a police officer has committed a crime. Black is the color of the assumption of criminality and without

3. Feldman, "NYPD Officer Daniel Pantaleo: I Didn't Put Garner In a Chokehold."

4. For instance according to the FBI "Crime in the United States 2013" report of known murders white on white murders = 83% and black on black murders = 90%.

a serious shake-up in the legal system there is little that can be done to change that color filter. This is why we chanted, "The whole damn system is guilty as hell!"

Defending this system by pointing to the "rule of law," the criminal justice system may seem logical to people for whom the system works. It is not a helpful argument for people, Black people, who are victims of this new caste system, as civil rights attorney and professor Michelle Alexander brilliantly argues in her book, *The New Jim Crow*.

> The fate of millions of people–indeed the future of the Black community itself–may depend on the willingness of those who care about racial justice to re-examine their basic assumptions about the role of the criminal justice system in our society. The fact that more than half of the young black men in many large American cities are currently under the control of the criminal justice system (or saddled with criminal records) is not–as many argue–just a symptom of poverty or poor choices, but rather evidence of a new racial caste system at work.[5]

Ending the new racial caste system will require intervention both from its creator, the federal government, and an outcry from the American public. Claims against racial profiling practices, a major police strategy, have been stymied and Alexander argues that successful challenges to this policy are not likely to continue in this current system because of one Supreme Court decision, called *Alexander v. Sandoval* in which the court "eliminat[ed] the last remaining avenue for challenging racial bias in the criminal justice system."[6] That one avenue was Title VI of the Civil Rights Act of 1964, which "prohibits federally funded programs or activities from discriminating on the basis of race."[7] Citizens who believe they have been victims of racial profiling must rely upon the federal government to bring charges under Title VI.

> Only the federal government can sue to enforce Title VI's antidiscrimination provisions–something it has neither the inclination nor the capacity to do in most racial profiling cases due to its limited resources and institutional reluctance to antagonize local law enforcement.[8]

5. Alexander, *New Jim Crow*, 16.

6. Ibid., 137.

7. Ibid., 138.

8. Ibid., 139.

In the face of sustained protests, the federal government has decided to launch a civil rights investigation of the Ferguson Police Department. The Department of Justice will review police practices over several years and will include the St. Louis county area making the scope of the investigation much broader than the Michael Brown killing. Within hours of the Staten Island grand jury decision not to indict the officers involved in Eric Garner's death, the Justice Department announced it would also begin a civil rights investigation into this unarmed Black man's death.

The plight of Black Americans against racially targeted police strategies is a crisis which womanist queer theology must address. Our commitment as womanists is to "the survival and wholeness of entire people, male and female."[9] The crisis in Ferguson has been a concrete test of that commitment as well as the significance of race, class, sex, and gender identity as womanist points of departure from Western theology.

The ongoing argument about whether race played any part in the killing of Michael Brown and Eric Garner simply means that America is primarily undecided about oppression and thus the deleterious forces of racism continue with impunity. The question of whether or not the police officers who killed Brown and Garner are racist is a zero sum game of distraction from the real issue of institutionalized racism deeply embedded within American institutions of power such as our municipal courts and police departments. A system that is corruptly racist is susceptible to hiring racists and employing strategies against the very citizens it ought protect and serve. In Ferguson and St. Louis County reported discriminatory practices included unequal market places, racial profiling leading to excessive traffic ticketing and costly warrants, public policies that create segregated communities,[10] redlining, and city revenues accumulated through the incarceration of Black and poor citizens.

Not only is America undecided about whether racism had any impact on the killing of Brown and Garner, but based upon the political editorials and comments left on online blog sites I wonder if Americans are not being intentionally miseducated about racism. If this is the case, what more can we say about racism? What teachable discourse can we offer to this historic conversation?

9. Walker, *In Search of Our Mothers' Gardens,* xi.

10. See Rothstein, "Making of Ferguson," 2014.

In the late 60s, Martin Luther King, Jr. defined racism as, "A doctrine of congenital inferiority and worthlessness of people."[11] On the personal level, racism is the belief in the "worthlessness" of a specific group of people. It is the myth that one group of people is superior to all other groups based upon the category of race. That is, the doctrine of racism purports that one's race determines human traits, behavior, and intelligence and that these factors also predetermine the individual's social and economic status in society. Though race has been proven not to be biological, the categorization of people based upon race, that is skin color, is commonplace in our society and institutions. As a belief, it is an internal cancer that diminishes the wonder and beauty of the human spirit.

When this belief of racism is acted upon to debase and/or discriminate another, it threatens the vitality of personal relationships and societal wellbeing. In America, institutional racism continues to be the primary instrument used to enforce personal racism. The success of our democracy depends upon ensuring that we stop the plague of racism within our educational, political, and legal systems. The leadership of one Black man as President of the United States is not indicative of the dissolution of institutional racism. What has been created and sustained for years by those who have a disproportionate share of American power and benefits–White people—will take years of meticulous deconstruction.

That task is being demanded on the streets of Ferguson, New York, Boston, Miami, and Berkeley. The ranks of protestors all across America consist of Black, White, Latino, and Asian people chanting, "Tell me what democracy looks like! This is what democracy looks like!" This is not a cry to suggest that democracy only looks like a mass gathering of people demanding justice. Rather, from my space amongst the protestors, I understood us as demanding that democracy must look like and work for all the people of this country.

A few other points about racism that I think are important for our times:

Watching and hearing the vitriol spewed by a few White bigots, some personally attacking me, pained but did not shock me. I'm accustomed to people–heterosexual and LGBTQ–who have not had their hearts transformed by the love of God making racist comments about Black people. I believe, very strongly, that they are fewer and fewer in number in this country. Nonetheless, the constant barrage of attacks that appears on social

11. King, *Where Do We Go From Here*, 48.

media against Black people when the word "racism" was invoked caused me to step back in order to reevaluate what we mean when we say "racism."

These days some no longer agree that racism is "prejudice plus power." The bleak days of the Great Recession took such a toll on people across the nation that the term "power" now seems to suggest only those who have amassed wealth. To wit, the current debate that addresses whether poor whites can actually be racist according to the "prejudice plus power" definition. At the individual level, it is better to think of racism as "prejudice plus discrimination based on the belief of the superiority of your race to all other races of people." In America we also need to add the ongoing benefits accrued on the basis of that discrimination: white privilege. All this said, while there may be some Blacks who despise and actually hate whites, they do not have the benefits of social, economic, and political privilege based on their race and a history of discrimination.

As a womanist, I can't abide hatred of any people. I wrote in an earlier chapter about guarding ourselves against a bitterness of our souls because I have experienced that bitterness and have watched people I love succumb to that bitterness after years of fighting against racism. I struggle with hatred because there is some behavior so heinous that hatred seems justifiable, for instance, when I read slave narratives and come across those entries of slaves yearning for the death of their slave owners or when I read about the joy slaves felt watching the murder of a paddyroller. It would be strange had no slave ever come to hate their oppressor. Nevertheless, our forebears survived slavery not on the basis of hatred and vengeance but on the basis of a sustained and righteous struggle for liberation.

Despite the experience of oppression, we cannot succumb to hatred. Every day we must work on our own pain with the same vigor that we work to eradicate the cause of our pain. When we sing, "We Shall Overcome," we must keep in mind that the journey towards true liberation begins each day, "deep in my heart."

Therefore ought we look seriously rediscover self-purification as a necessary preparatory and continuing step in any nonviolent protest? This process involves the willingness to make sacrifices to achieve the goal of liberation. "Are you able to accept blows without retaliating? Are you able to endure the ordeal of jail?"[12] If hatred is in our heart, we betray our own goals. If extremism is our character, we betray our fellow activists.

12. King, "Letter From a Birmingham Jail," 291.

Our womanist trait, as one who "loves the people" can actually be a helpful resource in these days of justice making and the increase of anarchists on the periphery of the current movement. They are misguided. They are opportunists engaged in public histrionics to score points off the struggle of Black persons for liberation and justice by "getting arrested" as a sign that they are "down" with the movement rather than being arrested as a result of civil disobedience. What is behind the strategy of civil disobedience? Is it not ultimately about disruption? To say, "We will do this and if we are to be arrested then let's fill the jails by our witness? Or, in the case of the Church to say, "We will perform same-sex marriages and if that means we will be brought to trial then let us fill the Church courts by our witness?"

Disruption of the system that holds on to the status quo, that refuses to relinquish its oppressive ways without confrontation. This is the methodology of the oppressed as they are fighting for liberation. Disruption of a system should not, however be equated with denigration of individuals and ratchet outbursts.

I had only to compare the scenes I filmed to know not everyone who marches as a protestor really had the ultimate demands of the movement in mind. As young leaders chanted, "Black Lives Matter!" opportunists and extremists threw rocks and other objects from behind the nonviolent protestors. As clergy groups and activists stood defiantly demanding justice before police clad in riot gear, some joined the marches displaying an out of place bravado and unwillingness to walk the way of peace. I saw, as I have seen in other liberation movements, beautiful determined resistance as well as inner turmoil brought on by those who aim for power and control. Amidst this tension is always the possibility that someone will be harmed and hatred will take root either towards the police or one another.

Hatred cannot be the price paid for justice nor can we allow co-opting and the dilution of the primary focus: #BlackLivesMatter.

I have written about Ferguson and the national protest to end militarized and excessive police force because the oppression of Black people demands the attention of womanist queer theology. Just as the young activist leaders have insisted that "#BlackLivesMatters includes Black LGBTQ lives," womanist theology has always insisted that Black lives matter to our scholarship. Womanist queer theology carries forth this precept in solidarity with Black communities, our cultural context, seeking justice and liberation of our people. The issues that affect the lives of Black people are critical also to our lives.

We queer those systems that are detrimental to the survival of an entire Black people. Like the young activists leaders, our goal is to disrupt, to deconstruct all that stands against the wellbeing of Black people. As womanists we take seriously the social location of Black women, the contributions of Black women and, sadly, the murder of Black women at the hands of criminal police forces.

The presence of Black women as leaders within this movement is of vital importance. Womanist queer theology must continue to chronicle their work and allow their narratives to teach us about survival, thriving, and demanding liberation. We also follow the progress of the movement by standing in opposition to any and all patriarchy.

We embrace "Black" knowing the baggage of essentialism that the category represents. Yet womanist queer theology argues that as a body of people, the lives that #BlackLivesMatter addresses have encountered microaggressions on the basis of this racial classification. We cannot be silent on this point.

Unlike the near erasure of the work of Black LGBT persons during the '60s civil rights movement, womanist queer scholarship will emphasize, as I have attempted here, the presence of Black LBTQ women at the forefront of this contemporary protest movement. The participation and leadership of Black women who self-identify as queer is an excellent response to one of the questions which I posed at the beginning of the writing: Does the definition and use of the term so radicalize its advocates that they end up self-segregating themselves from the rest of society? The answer, at this time is "no." Advocates have actually stepped into society challenging bigotry while proudly calling themselves queer.

At its best, queer theology pursues the ending of discrimination against LGBTQ persons. This is also the work of womanist queer theology with a special focus on the queer systems that serve as instruments of racism. Queer theory and queer theology must move out of the academy and onto the streets of our nation in solidarity with the oppressed and challenge the very idea of white superiority. This means following, *not* showing up demanding a position of leadership or that your voice be prominent.

Happily, many of our LGBTQ allies understand the significance of this era in our nation. They participate in the struggle as humble but resilient allies who recognize that the work to be done is not only about marriage equality or a fully inclusive Church. There are many dimensions to our work. Combatting racism is a necessary action for all LGBTQ persons who believe in freedom. Where racism affects Black people, it affects all LGBTQ persons not only because of Black LGBTQ persons but because justice is not really won until there is justice for all. If we really believe in one race, the human race, the crisis of #BlackLivesMatters is a crisis for all lives.

At the end of the day, eradicating oppression is the heart of queer womanist theological reflection. We must examine not just racism but sexism, not just homophobia but transphobia, not just poverty but war, and not just the fluidity of boundaries but the hegemony of the status quo. The efficacy of womanist queer theology will be its ability to be inclusive in its methodology, appreciative of its womanist history, and relevant in its scholarship, all towards the goal of helping usher in freedom and justice for all people.

As for an unyielding system? In the words of the protestors, "Shut. It. Down." In the academy this means being persistent against the demands to assimilate, to reduce our cultural learning in order to advocate white hegemony through what "should be taught" in the classroom. The subversive work of Black people living in America is as useful and necessary today as ever. That work does not stop when we enter the classroom, the church, or the several networks in which we exist. Shutting down oppression requires continued subversion, continued research to reveal injustice, and continued collaboration across different contexts. Oppression may always exist in our society, but it cannot be allowed to rule the day. To find the way forward from this perennial problem, Black lives must matter and it is the task of queer womanist scholarship to continue ensuring those lives includes Black lesbian, gay, bi-sexual, transgender and queer persons. Our lives do matter. Always.

Bibliography

Alexander, Michelle. *The New Jim Crow: Mass Incarceration in the Age of Colorblindness.* New York: The New Press, 2011.

ArchCity Defenders. "Municipal Courts Whitepaper." https://www.dropbox.com/s/vwptqn3mhq9xvy7/ArchCity%20Defenders%20Municipal%20Courts%20Whitepaper.pdf.

Asanti, Ta'Shia. "Black Lesbians & God: Our Search for Spirituality." *Lesbian News* 10 (1999) 26.

Augustine. *City of God.* 2 vols. Translated by Marcus Dods. Edinburgh: T. & T. Clark, 1921.

Baker, Ella. "Bigger Than a Hamburger." *The Southern Patriot.* June 1960. http://www.historyisaweapon.com/defcon1/bakerbigger.html.

Baldwin, James. "Negro Leaders on Violence." *Time Magazine,* August 20, 1965.

Barth, Karl. *Church Dogmatics II.1: The Doctrine of God.* Translated by T. H. L. Parker, W. B. Johnston, Harold Knight, and J. L. M. Haire. Edinburgh: T. & T. Clark, 1957.

Bates, D. Dionne. "Once-Married African-American Lesbians and Bisexual Women: Identity Development and the Coming-Out Process." *Journal of Homosexuality* 2 (2010) 211.

Battle, Juan J., and Natalie D. A. Bennett. "Striving for Place: Lesbian, Gay, Bisexual and Transgender (LGBT) People." In *A Companion to Post 1945 America,* edited by Jean-Christophe Agnew and Roy Rosenzweig, 416–17. Malden, MA: Blackwell, 2005.

The Book of Discipline of The United Methodist Church. Nashville: The United Methodist Publishing House, 2012.

The Book of Worship of the United Methodist Church. Nashville: The United Methodist Publishing House, 2012.

Butler, Judith. *Gender Trouble: Feminism and the Subversion of Identity.* New York: Routledge, 2006.

Cannon, Katie G. *Black Womanist Ethics.* 1988. Reprint, Eugene: Wipf & Stock, 2006.

Chauncey, George. *Gay New York: Gender, Urban Culture, and the Making of the Gay Male World, 1890–1940.* New York: Basic, 1994.

Copeland, M. Shawn. *Enfleshing Freedom: Body, Race, and Being.* Minneapolis: Fortress, 2010.

Culler, Jonathan D. *Ferdinand de Saussure.* Ithaca: Cornell University Press, 1986.

Douglas, Kelly Brown. *Sexuality and the Black Church.* New York: Orbis Books, 1999.

Ebony Magazine. "The Man Who Lived Thirty Years as a Woman," November 1975, 85–88.

FBI. "Crime in the United States." 2013. http://www.fbi.gov/about-us/cjis/ucr/crime-in-the-u.s/2013/crime-in-the-u.s.-2013/offenses-known-to-law-enforcement/expanded-homicide/expanded_homicide_data_table_6_murder_race_and_sex_of_vicitm_by_race_and_sex_of_offender_2013.xls.

FBI. "Hate Crime Statistics." 2012. http://www.fbi.gov/about-us/cjis/ucr/hate-crime/2012/topic-pages/victims/victims_final.

FBI. "National Incident Based Reporting System." 2012. http://www.fbi.gov/about-us/cjis/ucr/nibrs/2012/data-tables.

Feldman, Josh. "NYPD Officer Daniel Pantaleo: I Didn't Put Garner In a Chokehold." *Mediaite*, December 11, 2014. http://www.mediaite.com/online/nypd-officer-daniel-pantaleo-i-didnt-put-garner-in-a-chokehold/.

Follman, Mark. "Michael Brown's Mom Laid Flowers Where He Was Shot—And Police Crushed Them." 2014. http://www.motherjones.com/politics/2014/08/ferguson-st-louis-police-tactics-dogs-michael-brown?utm_source=huffingtonpost.com&utm_medium=referral&utm_campaign=pubexchange_article.

Foucault, Michel. *The History of Sexuality: An Introduction, Vol. 1*. New York: Random House, 1978.

Goldman, Roger, and David Gallen. *Thurgood Marshall, Justice for All*. New York: Carroll & Graf, 1992.

Goodman, J. David. "Difficult Decisions Ahead in Responding to Police Chokehold Homicide." *New York Times*, August 4, 2014. http://www.nytimes.com/2014/08/05/nyregion/after-eric-garner-chokehold-prosecuting-police-is-an-option.html?_r=0.

Grant, Jacquelyn. *White Women's Christ and Black Women's Jesus: Feminist Christology and Womanist Response*. Atlanta: Scholars, 1989.

Hill, Renée. "Who Are We For Each Other? Sexism, Sexuality, and Womanist Theology." In *Black Theology: A Documentary History*, rev. ed., 2 vols., edited by James Cone and Gayraud Wilmore, 2:345–51. Maryknoll: Orbis, 1993.

The Intersex Society of North America. "What is Intersex?" http://www.isna.org/faq/what_is_intersex

Johnson, Thomas. "Ezell Ford: The Mentally Ill Black Man Killed By the LAPD Two Days After Michael Brown's Death." *The Washington Post*, August 15, 2014. http://www.washingtonpost.com/news/morning-mix/wp/2014/08/15/ezell-ford-the-mentally-ill-black-man-killed-by-the-lapd-two-days-after-michael-browns-death/.

Jordan, June. *Affirmative Acts: Political Essays*. New York: Anchor, 1998.

Kant, Immanuel. *Critique of Pure Reason*. Translated and edited by Paul Guyer. New York: Cambridge University Press, 1998.

King, Martin Luther, Jr. *Where Do We Go From Here: Chaos or Community?* Boston: Beacon Press, 1968.

———. *A Testament of Hope: The Essential Writings and Speeches of Martin Luther King, Jr.* Edited by James M. Washington. New York: HarperCollins, 1986.

Lorde, Audre. *Sister Outsider: Essays and Speeches*. Freedom: Crossing, 1984.

MacPherson, John. *Westminster Confession of Faith*. Edinburgh: T. & T. Clark, 1881.

Maslow, Abraham H. "A Theory of Motivation." *Psychological Review* 50 (1943) 370–96.

Miller, David. "Empiricism and Process Theology: God is What God Does." *Christian Century*, March 1976, 284–87.

Mitchell-Kernan, Claudia. "Signifying, Loud-talking and Marking." In *Signifyin(g), Sanctifyin, and Slam Dunking*, edited by Gena Dagel Caponi, 309–30. Amherst: The University of Massachusetts Press, 1999.

BIBLIOGRAPHY

Mock, Janet. *Redefining Realness: My Path to Womanhood, Identity, Love and So Much More*. New York: Atria. 2014.

Morrison, Toni. *Beloved*. New York: Random House, 2006.

Moya, Paula M. L., and Michael R. Hames-García, eds. *Reclaiming Identity: Realist Theory and the Predicament of Postmodernism*. Los Angeles: University of California Press, 2000.

Murray, Pauli. Papers. Schlesinger Library, Radcliff Institute, Harvard University, 1898.

Niebuhr, Reinhold. *The Nature and Destiny of Man. A Christian Interpretation, Volume 1: Human Nature*. Louisville: Westminster John Knox, 1996.

NVAVP Report: 2012 Lesbian, Gay, Bisexual, Transgender, Queer and HIV-Affected Hate Violence in 2012. http://www.avp.org/storage/documents/2013_ncavp_hvreport_final.pdf.

Palm Beach County History Online. "School Desegregation." http://www.pbchistoryonline.org/page/school-desegregation

Parker, William. Interview with *New York Times*, August 1965, 8.

PBS.org. "Timeline: Milestones in the American Gay Rights Movement." http://www.pbs.org/wgbh/americanexperience/features/timeline/stonewall/.

Pew Forum. "A Religious Portrait of African Americans," January 30, 2009. http://www.pewforum.org/2009/01/30/a-religious-portrait-of-african-americans/.

Raboteau, Albert. *Slave Religion: The "Invisible Institution" in the Antebellum South*. New York: Oxford University Press, 2004.

Ransby, Barbara. *Ella Baker and the Black Freedom Movement: A Radical Democratic Vision*. Chapel Hill: The University of North Carolina Press, 2003.

Riggs, Marcia. "Living as Religious Ethical Mediators: A Vocation for People of Faith in the Twenty-First Century." In *Womanist Theological Ethics: A Reader*, edited by Katie Geneva Cannon et al., 250. Louisville: Westminster Knox, 2011.

Roosevelt, Eleanor. "Some of My Best Friends are Negro." *Ebony Magazine* (1975) 73–78.

Rothstein, Richard. "The Making of Ferguson: Public Policies at the Root of Its Troubles." Report on Inequality and Poverty for the Economic Policy Institute. October 15, 2014. http://www.epi.org/publication/making-ferguson/#how-ferguson-became-ferguson.

Ruso, Nazenin. "Jacques Derrida and Deconstruction," *Philosophy Now* 60 (2013). https://philosophynow.org/issues/60/A_Position_On_Derrida.

Sanders, Cheryl. "Roundtable Discussion: Christian Ethics and Theology in Womanist Perspective." *Journal of Feminist Studies in Religion* 2 (1989) 83–112.

Saussure, Ferdinand de. *Course in General Linguistics*. Translated by Wade Baskin. Edited by Perry Meisel and Haun Saussy. New York: Columbia University Press, 1959.

Sheppard, Phillis Isabella. *Self, Culture and Others in Womanist Practical Theology*. New York: Palgrave MacMillan, 2011.

Steinmetz, Katy. "Laverne Cox Talks to TIME about the Transgender Movement." *Time.com*, May 29, 2104. http://time.com/132769/transgender-orange-is-the-new-black-laverne-cox-interview/.

Terkel, Amanda. "Police Officer Caught on Video Calling Protestors 'F***ing Animals." *The Huffington Post*, August 12, 2014. http://www.huffingtonpost.com/2014/08/12/michael-brown-protests_n_5672163.html.

Thomas, Linda E. "Womanist Theology, Epistemology, and a New Anthropological Paradigm." In *Living Stones in the Household of God: The Legacy and Future of Black Theology*, edited Linda E. Thomas, 37–49. Minneapolis: Augsburg Fortress, 2004.

Thurman, Howard. *A Strange Freedom: The Best of Howard Thurman*. Boston: Beacon Press, 1999.

Townes, Emilie M. *In a Blaze of Glory: Womanist Spirituality as a Social Witness*. Nashville: Abingdon, 1995.

Truth, Sojourner. "When Women Gets Her Rights Man Will Be Right." In *Words of Fire: An Anthology of African-American Feminist Thought*, edited by Beverly Guy-Sheftall, 38. New York: The New Press, 1867.

———. "Ain't I a Woman?" 1851. Women's Rights National Historic Park. http://www.nps.gov/wori/historyculture/sojourner-truth.htm.

Valdés, Mario J. "Binary Opposition." In *Encyclopedia of Contemporary Literary Theory: Approaches, Scholars, Terms*, edited by Irene Rima Makaryk, 511. Toronto: University of Toronto Press, 1993.

Walker, Alice. *In Search of Our Mothers' Gardens: Womanist Prose*. Orlando: Harcourt Brace & Company, 1983.

Warner, Michael. "Introduction: Fear of a Queer Planet." *Social Text* 29 (1991) 3–17.

Wilkins, Kimberly "Sweet Brown." *Oklahoma City News* interview, April 10, 2012. http://kfor.com/2012/04/08/okc-apartment-complex-catches-fire-5-units-damaged/.

"Yvette Flunder, Dispelling the Myth." YouTube video, 44:31. Posted by Bishop Adjutant, November 29, 2014. https://www.youtube.com/watch?v=hlp7lswnNDc.